...t's Wrong with My Snake?

By *John Rossi, DVM, MA*
and Roxanne Rossi

lumina
MEDIA

Jarelle S. Stein, *Editor*
Cover and layout design concept by Michael Vincent Capozzi
Indexed by Melody Englund

Front and back cover photos by Greg Graziani.
The additional photos in this book are by John Rossi, pp. 5–6, 10, 14, 17,
19–20, 23, 27–31, 34–35, 37–40, 43, 46, 51–56 (top), 57–60, 62–23, 66,
68–70, 72–73, 78–79, 82 (bottom), 91–94, 99–101, 103, 105, 112, 114,
117–119, 121–123, 125, 138, 140–141; Paul Freed, 8, 11, 15–16, 18,
21–22, 24, 32–33, 42, 44, 48–50, 56 (bottom), 76, 81–82 (top), 84, 87,
89–90, 96, 98, 106, 108, 111, 115, 126, 130–131, 133; Don Swerida, 55,
64, 74, 102, 132; James Gerholdt, 83

LCCN: 96-183295
ISBN: 1-882770-84-6
ISBN 13: 978-188277084-7

2030 Main Street, Suite 1400
Irvine, CA 92614
www.facebook.com/luminamediabooks
www.luminamedia.com

CONTENTS

Acknowledgments 4

Introduction 5

1: Selection and Acclimation 7

2: Disease and the Captive Environment 37

3: Skin 48

4: Stomatitis 59

5: Parasites 62

6: Gastrointestinal Problems 72

7: Feeding Problems 81

8: Reproduction 98

9: Respiratory Problems 112

10: Neurological Problems 117

11: Sudden Death 120

12: Pediatrics 123

13: Geriatrics 127

14: Psychological Factors 130

15: Choosing a Veterinarian 138

16: Medicines 141

References 150

Additional Reading 153

Index 154

About the Authors 160

ACKNOWLEDGMENTS

The authors wish to thank Steve Barten, DVM, and Roger Klingenberg, DVM, for their support and photographic contributions. Thanks to Pat Grace, University of Florida Extension agent, for suggestions regarding the management of escape.

INTRODUCTION

Snakes are among the fastest growing groups of captive animals in the United States. Although even today many people loathe these slithering animals, snakes have become the focus of an increasing number of herpetoculturists. This recent rise of the popularity of snakes can be attributed to their striking beauty, fascinating movements, interesting behaviors, and docile temperaments (with most species) as well as their ease of care and handling. As the number of snakes in captivity has increased, so has awareness of their requirements and medical problems. Veterinarians, confronted with a growing number of reptile patients, have made tremendous progress in the field of herpetological medicine over the past ten years.

Although there are several technical reference books on the veterinary treatment of reptiles, there are few user-friendly home medical references dealing specifically with the common medical problems of snakes and their treatment. The authors have compiled this concise, easy-to-use

The ball python is among the most popular pet snakes. Because it is small and nonaggressive, it is a good pet for beginners. However, the ball python is prone to parasitism and anorexia.

manual to fill an important gap in the popular herpeto-cultural literature. We begin with a general discussion of selection and acclimation. In this overview, we present the important considerations in choosing a species that suits your experience level as well as in selecting a potentially healthy specimen. We discuss the signs of disease, stress, and health problems associated with acclimation. Then we'll discuss how disease relates to the captive environment and the most common medical problems of captive snakes. There also are sections on problems associated with very young snakes, very old snakes, gravid snakes, and escaped snakes and discussions of emergency treatments for overheated snakes. Look to the chapters on psychological factors and sudden death for explanations of unusual behaviors. A medicine chart is included to help veterinarians dose snakes properly, in case they are inexperienced with these animals. To close the book, several charts are

Herpetologist Versus Herpetoculturist

Herpetoculturists are interested in keeping and breeding reptiles and amphibians of all types to fulfill personal needs and goals as well as for commercial purposes. Herpetologists study reptiles and amphibians from a more scientific view and are not necessarily interested in keeping reptiles in captivity or breeding them. Some herpetologists are, of course, herpetoculturists.

provided to help veterinarians inexperienced with these animals to properly diagnose health problems and to determine the correct dosage of common medicines used in herpetological practice.

In general, this book focuses on disease prevention and presents the many aspects of proper husbandry that help prevent the onset of health problems before they become serious and, in some cases, untreatable.

CHAPTER 1

SELECTION AND ACCLIMATION

There seems to be an endless array of snakes available for purchase. These animals come in all different shapes, sizes, and colors. There are exotics and natives, melanistics and albinos, young and old, rare and common, expensive and cheap, males and females, captive-bred and wild-caught. How do you choose the best snake for you, and is there really a "best" pet snake?

General Selection Considerations

With nearly three thousand species of snakes in existence and hundreds of these presently available as pets, there is no one best captive snake. Many species seem to adapt readily to captivity and eat commonly available food items, such as domestic rodents, whereas other species seem to adapt poorly to captivity or require food items not

The Mexican vine snake is an arboreal snake with special housing and dietary requirements. Always research a snake's needs before purchasing it.

readily available. It would seem logical, therefore, to choose a snake from the first group, unless you are very experienced in the captive care, husbandry, and maintenance of difficult snakes or have a great deal of time and money to invest in maintaining one of these species. For most people, ease of maintenance is the primary consideration in determining whether to keep a particular species. Following this factor, consider the qualities discussed below.

Adult Size
Give careful consideration to the adult size of the snake species you are selecting. For most people, medium to large snakes are better suited for keeping in a home vivarium than the giant snakes are. Burmese pythons (*Python molurus bivittatus*) and green anacondas (*Eunectes murinus*), although cute when young, easily grow to more than 10 feet (3 meters) long within their first two years and ultimately reach a length of 20 feet (6 m) or more. Where will you house one of these snakes? Is it even legal in your state to own such a large snake? (Always check with your local government to find out about regulations that may control or restrict snake keeping in your area. See also the box in the following section on snake families for an overview of reptile keeping guidelines established by the American Federation of Herpetoculturists.)

It is generally easier to maintain a captive-bred adult snake than a juvenile because many juveniles have difficulty feeding. If you do purchase a juvenile, make sure it is feeding before you bring it home.

Disposition

What is the disposition of the species you are considering? Although temperament appears to be an individual trait, there are certain species that tend to be more aggressive than others. Arboreal boas (*Corallus* spp.) have a reputation for aggression, and many of these snakes seem quite willing to bite their keepers.

Sex

In captivity, female snakes are generally more aggressive feeders than males are. The reason is unknown, but we suspect that it may be related to higher energy demands that females have for reproduction. This would suggest that female snakes would be easier to keep than males; however, males have a lower risk of problems associated with reproduction.

Origin

A common question is whether to purchase a captive-bred (born in captivity, usually meaning intentionally bred by a professional snake breeder) or a wild-caught (imported) snake. Wild-caught specimens are usually heavily parasitized and must be treated to remove these parasites. Wild-caught snakes may not adapt well to captivity; such specimens are subject to higher stress levels, which tend to suppress immunity and can lead to additional health problems, such as various infections and gastrointestinal problems and even an increased risk of tumors. For these reasons, captive-bred snakes are almost always preferable to wild-caught specimens. Selecting captive-bred snakes also reduces the demand for capture and importation of wild-caught snakes, thereby helping to preserve them in their natural habitat.

Age

A snake's age may be an important factor. The young of some species, such as the gray-banded kingsnake (*Lampropeltis alterna*), are notoriously difficult to get started feeding. For this reason, many experts advise purchasing adults or a well-started juvenile, that is, a specimen already feeding regularly. Even though well-started juveniles may be more expensive, the difference in the ease of acclimation may be well worth the additional cost. With other species, however, it's easier to acclimate a young captive-bred snake than an imported adult, as is the case, for example, with ball pythons.

Thoroughly research the species you have selected to make the best decision at the time of purchase.

The blood python is a medium-size, richly colored snake. Despite its calm appearance, a blood python can be aggressive.

Appearance (Color Pattern)

The absolute last characteristic to use in determining whether to purchase a particular snake is its appearance. A snake may be beautiful, but if it is difficult to keep, is aggressive, or grows to a very large adult size, it probably will be a source of grief to its owner and thus will be much less likely to thrive in captivity. A snake in this position is, unfortunately, more likely to be abandoned or, even worse, given to another owner who is not prepared for the challenge of caring for a poorly acclimated, stressed snake. Resist the urge to purchase a snake purely on the basis of its appearance. The animal's temperament and health are far more important factors when making the important decision of which snake to purchase.

Snake Families

One can make some generalizations about the requirements of snakes in captivity by knowing a little about how herpetologists have classified them taxonomically. The family Boidae, for example, comprises constrictor snakes of three subfamilies—the pythons, the boas, and the sand boas. Boidae is largely tropical (most species in this family require fairly high temperatures and humidity levels) and largely arboreal (most species require large enclosures that support sturdy branches to coil around). The rubber boa and rosy boa are exceptions to this rule; they are small terrestrial snakes that can be exposed to cooler temperatures safely. The family Colubridae is a huge group of snakes (approximately 1,700 species) with a worldwide distribution. Perhaps the main generalization about this group is that most species are small in size, making them more manageable in captivity for keepers with limited space or funds.

Boids

Members of the family Boidae (the boids, for short) include some of the most popular and easy-to-maintain species. The following is an overview.

- **Small species:** Common species include ball pythons, green tree pythons, rainbow boas, rosy boas, rubber boas, sand boas, and spotted pythons. The ball python, when raised from a hatchling or yearling, is among the most highly recommended of pet snakes. It adapts well to captivity and remains relatively small in size. It is slow moving and is easy to handle compared with other snake species. The

Although small snakes are usually easier to keep than large ones, that is not the case with the green tree python. It has special maintenance needs and may bite; only experienced herpetoculturists should own one.

ball python is beautiful in its normal (wild-type) pattern, though many stunning color morphs are available in the pet trade. The green tree python is recommended only for more experienced herpetoculturists; this species is more likely to bite than the other species in the group.

- **Large species:** Common species include blood pythons, boa constrictors, carpet pythons, and West Indian boas (*Epicrates* spp.). Of the large snakes, Colombian boa constrictors are the most recommended for keepers who want a large pet snake; these boas are usually docile, hardy snakes that can thrive even in suboptimal conditions, making them quite easy to care for. Borneo blood pythons and carpet pythons raised from hatchlings tend to become docile over time.

- **Very large species:** African rock pythons, Asian rock pythons, amethystine pythons, Burmese pythons, green anacondas, reticulated pythons, and water pythons are the most widely available of all large snakes. Statistically, the two most dangerous species in captivity are the reticulated python and the African rock python. The main difficulty with very large species is that herpetoculturists use improper methods for feeding and handling them. The aggressiveness of some very large species, such as anacondas, requires extra caution during handling to minimize the risk of accidents and other problems. At least two people are required to safely handle the adults of very large species. The now defunct, but once pioneering, American Federation of Herpetoculturists established guidelines for the keeping of large boas and pythons. An updated version of these guidelines appears in the following box.

Colubrids

The larger, constricting, rodent-eating members of the family Colubridae (the colubrids, for short) are among the most popular and easy to keep of all snakes. Popular and readily available species include Baird's rat snakes, corn snakes, fox snakes, gopher snakes, kingsnakes, milk snakes, North

Snake Keeping Guidelines from the American Federation of Herpetoculturists

The following guidelines for the responsible keeping of large constrictors have been presented at several public hearings and served as models for sound regulation. The authors strongly suggest that snake keepers follow these suggestions to help preserve the herpetocultural hobby.

- In consideration of the right of the public to not unexpectedly be exposed to snakes such as large constrictors, and realizing the irresponsible behaviors demonstrated by some snake owners, it is recommended that no snake shall be openly displayed in a public setting outside of proper and established forums, such as herpetological shows, educational displays, pet stores, and events whereby members of the public are forewarned that snakes may be openly displayed.

- All large snakes must be housed in secure enclosures with either hinged doors, sliding tops, or sliding glass fronts that include a locking mechanism. Such enclosures should preferably be contained in a room modified to prevent snake escapes and with a door that shall be kept shut or locked when the room is not occupied by the owners. As herpetoculturists, we all benefit from practices that prevent the escape of pet snakes.

- All snakes must be transported in a manner that prevents the possibility of escape. They shall be contained in a sturdy cloth bag free of holes or tears and placed inside a box or similar container with holes for aeration. The container should then be sealed or locked shut. Care must be taken to use cloth bags with a weave that allows for adequate air exchange. When shipping snakes by air, the airlines must be consulted as to their packing requirements.

- When handling or performing maintenance of any of the giant snakes more than 8 feet (2.4 m) (green anacondas, Asian rock pythons including Burmese pythons, African rock pythons, reticulated pythons, and scrub pythons), another person should be present or at least within easy calling range. An additional person should be present for every additional 4 feet (1.2 m) of snake, that is, two people when handling or maintaining a 12-foot (3.7-m) python.

- No boids (pythons and boas) that can achieve an adult length more than 8 feet should ever be owned by or sold to minors.

- As with other potentially dangerous animals, such as dogs, owners of large constrictors should be aware that they can be liable for the medical costs of treating injuries as well as additional financial damages.

American rat snakes, pine snakes, and Trans Pecos rat snakes. In terms of docility, corn snakes (*Elaphe guttata* var.) and common kingsnakes (*Lampropeltis getula* var.) are among the most recommended species.

Milk snakes are among the most beautiful of these snakes, but most varieties are too active to recommend for keepers who choose to frequently handle their pets. (Exceptions include Andesian and Sinaloan milk snakes.) North American rat snakes (*Elaphe obsoleta*) are hardy, but their docility will vary among subspecies. Captive-raised black rat snakes and gray rat snakes are among the most docile, whereas Texas rat snakes may remain nippy even when raised in captivity. Fox snakes (*Elaphe vulpine* and *E. gloydii*) tend to be consistently docile but are somewhat more difficult to keep than other rat snakes because of their strong hibernation instincts. Gopher and pine snakes are active when handled, but they tend to be docile and are among the most impressive and most underappreciated of the North American colubrids. Larger colubrid species, such as some varieties of rat snakes and pine snakes, require more food and larger food items than some of the smaller species.

Natricines

Natricinae (natricines, for short), a subfamily of family Colubridae, include the popular garter snakes and the not-so-popular water snakes. Garter snakes are small, attractive animals that can be housed (individually) in fairly small enclosures—24 to 36 inches (61 to 91 centimeters)—and fed readily available prey items. Water snakes can be kept in a similar manner, but they are more likely to bite. We highly recommend natricines for beginners as well as for more experienced hobbyists. Selective breeding of rare morphs, such as albino checkered and Florida garter snakes and albino water snakes, has caused a renewed and fast-growing interest in this group of snakes.

Handling Snakes for Examination or Treatment

When we handle snakes for fun, we generally exercise little or no restraint. Often, we allow a snake to glide freely over our hands or arms, and sometimes we allow it to wrap around an arm or leg. However, handling a snake to administer treatment for a medical problem or to perform a physical examination requires restraint. You can restrain most small, nonvenomous snakes by grasping them firmly but gently behind the head, near the angle of the jaws, while supporting the body with your other hand.

Larger snakes generally require more support; five or more people may be needed to restrain a large snake for a physical examination or an injection. Large constrictors—such as pythons, anacondas, and some boas—are very powerful snakes, and an uninformed novice may be

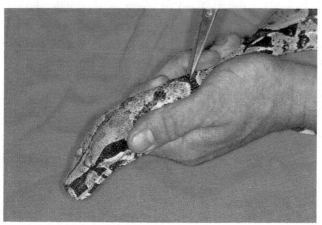

It's important to properly restrain your snake when it is being examined. Snakes can be easily injured if they are mishandled.

Always have an assistant when handling any snake more than 8 feet long. Large snakes are very powerful and can be dangerous for a single handler.

unaware of how dangerous these species can be. As a general rule, have an assistant present to handle a constricting snake longer than 8 feet (2.4 m) and an another person for each additional 4 feet (1.2 m) of snake. A thorough physical examination may require two people to restrain a snake while a third person examines the animal.

A number of devices have been used to assist in the restraint of snakes for a physical examination or for other purposes. These include Plexiglas tubes, foam rubber pads,

Caution!

Because snakes and other reptiles have a single occipital condyle (meaning only one part of the skull is in contact with the first neck vertebra), they are particularly susceptible to cervical dislocation. Therefore, you must exercise extreme caution when handling snakes that struggle or twist vigorously.

plastic pressboard, or a snake bag (a pillowcase is a less expensive option). If using a snake bag, you can keep one end of the snake in the bag while you examine the other end or administer injections. Even though plastic tubes and foam rubber pads are commonly used for venomous snakes, they are also excellent for restraining aggressive or uncooperative nonvenomous snakes. The snake is maneuvered into the tube, after which the tube and the snake are grasped and held together. If you are using a foam mat, gently place the snake upon the mat, then press the snake against the mat, using a clear shield. This procedure allows a careful examination, measurement, or treatment to be accomplished with some ease.

To examine a snake, first observe it from a distance, looking at overall appearance, ease of breathing, and luster of the skin. If it is moving about the cage, a healthy snake is alert and moving with good muscular and motor control. A healthy and alert snake will flick out its tongue often to get a sense of its surroundings. Examine the cage for stools; healthy stools are solid and normal in color, whereas loose,

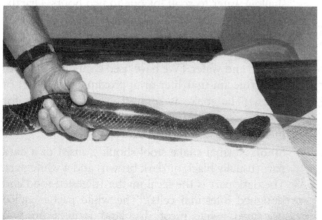

Plastic tubes are commonly used when handling venomous snakes such as this rattlesnake. They are also useful when handling any uncooperative snake.

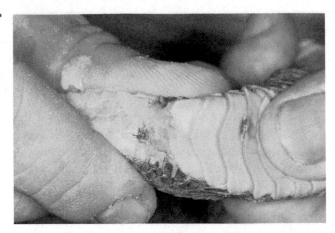

watery, foul-smelling stools indicate possible illness. The following guidelines will help you determine whether your snake is healthy or is in need of medical treatment or additional time in quarantine. (See also chapters 3, 5, and 6 for more detailed information on skin problems, parasites, and gastrointestinal problems.)

- **Mites:** Mites appear as tiny, beadlike creatures crawling on the scales and around the eye rims. You may see actual mites crawling on your hands immediately after you've handled an infected snake. Or you may observe silvery, white flecks on the scales—these are mite feces. Some experienced reptile veterinarians advise immediately putting a snake into a pan of shallow water to soak for one to two hours. Dry the snake, and place it in a quarantine cage (as described below). Another variation of mite treatment that we regularly use is to spray the snakes heavily with ivermectin and water. (We have used a mixture of 0.5 cc of ivermectin in 1 liter or approximately 1 quart of water.) The snake is sprayed every three days for three weeks minimum. (Parasite detection and treatment is discussed further in chapter 5.)

- **Stool:** Normal snake stool should consist of a dark part (usually black or dark brown) and a white part. The dark part is the fecal matter (digested food and sloughed intestinal cells). The white part is called uric acid, what most dry land reptiles produce instead of urea. Because uric acid is insoluble in water, it helps the reptiles to conserve body water. Stool that is watery, mucus laden, blood tinged, or greenish or yellowish may signal a problem.

- **Head and face:** Check the rostral (nose) area and mouth for abrasions. Hold the snake behind its head with one hand (while supporting the body on a table or using your arm to hold the snake against your body). With your other hand, gently pull the skin underneath the lower jaw to open the snake's mouth. The mouth should be clean, uniformly colored (usually pink, but white or blue in some species), and free of excessive amounts of mucus. The eyes should be bright, clear, and alertly moving to examine the environment. The tongue should flick regularly. Check the nares (nostrils) and heat-sensing pits, if they are present. These areas should be free of dried mucus plugs and parasites. The snake should breathe easily, without wheezing, open-mouth breathing, puffing of the throat, bubble blowing, or constant head elevation.

- **Skin:** Examine the skin, working from the head toward the tail, then looking at the vent on the underside. The skin should be smooth and shiny, free of lumps, abrasions, wounds, and discoloration. (Many species have keeled scales, which have a raised ridge running down the scale's center, that attribute to a rougher feel than smooth scales.) Check for the

If possible, let the snake slither over your hands and arms. The snake's body should not flatten as it does this. Flattening can indicate a malnourished animal.

presence of mites, especially between the scales and near the eyes and nostrils.

- **Body:** Next, gently run your fingers along the abdomen of the snake. You should not feel any firm masses. The cloacal area should be clean with a pink interior, without dried blood or caked mucus or fecal matter present. Ask to handle the snake (if it is nonvenomous). The body should feel strong and supple. As it crawls over your fingers, hands, or arms, the snake's body in most cases should not noticeably flatten. Flattening could indicate poor muscle tone and perhaps long-term anorexia.

Abnormalities may signal an illness. Although some health problems may be easy to correct, others may be difficult and require a lot of time and money on the keeper's part.

Transporting Your Snake

Improper transportation is among the major causes of disease and death among captive snakes. Failure to properly insulate the containers holding these reptiles during transport may result in either overheating or chilling of the animals, either of which may lead to illness or even death of the snakes. Five minutes in direct sunlight may be all it takes to kill a confined snake (even a heat-loving, diurnal snake), and a brief chill may result in fatal pneumonia.

A dog carrier works well to transport this Burmese python; a duffel bag also works well for a large snake. A pillowcase works great for smaller snakes.

Generally, snakes are best transported in clean cloth sacks, such as pillowcases. Place crumpled newspapers in the pillowcase to cushion the snake and protect it from trauma. Tie the neck of the pillowcase in a knot (first being certain that the snake is not in the area about to be tied). Small snakes (large snakes don't need this) may benefit from the addition of shredded newspaper that has been misted with water, which helps keep them from becoming dehydrated. Then place the sack inside a Styrofoam container into which you have punched several small air holes. For shipping purposes (meaning shipping by air, not short-term transport via car), place the Styrofoam container inside a cardboard box clearly marked with the destination address and, in large letters, "Live Animals! Avoid Extreme Heat or Cold." Punch air holes in the cardboard box as well. Reptiles are best shipped by express air freight. (Delta Air Lines, for example, has offered a reliable service for this purpose.) Venomous reptiles require additional packaging, usually double wooden, metal-rimmed crates. Contact your shipper for specific requirements.

Professional shippers usually send reptiles at night during hot weather and during the day in cold weather so that the animals are less likely to be exposed to extreme temperatures. Professionals also call the person receiving the shipment before sending the package to make sure someone will be at the airport waiting for it. This procedure shortens the duration of the snakes' crowded condition, lessening stress and improving their chances of survival. Shippers may enclose heat-producing packs (found in sporting goods stores) when shipping reptiles in the winter and cool packs or plastic containers containing ice when shipping reptiles in the summer.

Place your new snakes in their quarantine cages immediately upon receipt and offer them water. (See the following section on quarantine.) There is no telling how long these animals have been deprived of water; a few more hours without water could spell the difference between life and death for your snake. Dispose of the shipping crate and bags right away. If you want to save the bags for future use, immediately wash them with bleach to avoid the risk of a mite outbreak in a collection.

One last warning is in order: while driving with snakes in a car (properly secured in a locking container, of course), you must keep them out of direct sunlight. Coolers that plug into your car's cigarette lighter are superb devices for safely transporting snakes in a car, especially on a hot day. Just be careful they don't get too cold! Coolers, however, are

Professional shippers usually ship during the most temperate times of the day: warm nights and cool days. A good shipper does not leave snakes in shipping containers for long periods.

Always use a thermometer to gauge the temperature when transporting snakes.

no match for direct sunlight. Neither are tents, cars, or even houses in many cases. Be sure the cooler or other transportation container is kept in a shaded part of your vehicle and that you monitor the temperature inside the container. A good precaution for safe travel is to use a digital, battery-operated, indoor-outdoor thermometer with a probe to monitor the temperature inside the container. This device has saved the lives of a number of snakes in our care. (See chapter 2 for a discussion on heating and cooling devices.)

Snake Recognition and Identification

Unfortunately, one of the difficulties of keeping snakes in captivity today is preventing them from being stolen and identifying them if they escape. Identification will be much easier if your snake has been marked in such a way that there is no question about its ownership. In the past, keepers marked snakes by tattooing them or clipping some of their scales. Some photographed snakes to record distinctive patterns. Although these methods work, the latest and best way of identifying snakes is to use an implantable microchip (transponder). A number of veterinarians have successfully marked snakes for zoos and private breeders by using microchips, which are safe and rarely cause any problems, such as local infection or migration of the chip to an area where it will affect the snake's normal function. The most commonly used microchips for pet identification now are by AVID. The chips, which are no larger than a grain of rice,

This passive integrated transponder (PIT) tag is about the size of a grain of rice. Like dogs and cats, pet snakes are now receiving microchips to identify them in case they escape or are stolen.

are injected subcutaneously in most large snakes, via a large-gauge needle. In small snakes, the transponder may be carefully injected intraperitoneally (into the smooth, thin lining of the abdominal cavity); care must be taken to avoid major organs and blood vessels.

Personal Hygiene

Snakes may harbor bacteria or parasites that may be contagious to their owners as well as to other snakes in an established collection. We advise you to exercise caution when handling or cleaning up after these animals. Keep new arrivals isolated from those established in a collection for a period of two to three months, generally referred to as the quarantine period.

The most important precaution you can take is to practice good personal hygiene. Anytime you handle a snake (or any other animal), you must thoroughly wash your hands, preferably with an antibacterial soap. Even if you use regular hand soap, the physical act of washing will remove many potential pathogenic organisms. Liquid soap is better than bar soap because bacteria can survive on the bar and the soap holder. Anyone with wounds or abrasions on his or her hands should cover both hands with disposable latex gloves prior to handling snakes.

Never eat, drink, smoke, or bring your hands near your face after handling a snake without first washing your hands. Consider everything you touch while handling your snakes as possibly contaminated: pens, pencils, books— even the doorknobs in your snake room. The same rules apply for the handling of snake food items, especially rodents and amphibians, which are known to carry parasites contagious to people.

Grier and colleagues (1993) suggest that reptiles may be used in classroom situations with small children, but hand washing is mandatory after any contact with the animals. Make sure to encourage children to practice good hygiene. Keep toddlers and snakes well apart unless an adult is present to thoroughly wash children's hands after contact with the snake. Young children, elderly people, and otherwise immunocompromised individuals (those with impaired or weakened immune systems) are especially at risk of infection from some of the bacteria and parasites carried by snakes; we recommend very strict sanitation procedures— or even total avoidance—in these cases.

If possible, do not clean snake cages or cage accessories in a sink where dishes are washed or food is prepared. If you use a bathroom sink or tub, make sure to thoroughly disinfect the entire area afterward. Refrigerators and freezers housing food intended for human consumption are not appropriate locations for the storage of frozen rodents, amphibians, or feeder snakes. Although freezing may kill some parasites, it will not kill all the parasites that may be in these animals. Kitchen counters and other areas used for preparing food for people should also be off limits for reptiles and their food items, cages, and accessories.

Find a veterinarian who is familiar with snakes to perform physical and fecal exams on every snake you have. Check with local herp clubs or associations, such as the Association of Reptile and Amphibian Veterinarians, to find a specialist in your area. Fecal cultures to check for potentially communicable bacteria are advisable, particularly when small children or immunocompromised individuals will be in contact with the reptiles. These diagnostic tests may detect organisms that could affect you and your snake; early detection and treatment protect both of you. Some

Snakes kept in over-crowded, unsanitary conditions are likely to be infested with parasites. Always purchase snakes from reputable sources.

diseases, such as pentastomiasis and salmonellosis, are not treatable in snakes or not advisable to treat at this time. The diagnosis of such diseases, which have a potential to transfer from snakes to people, is often regarded as grounds for the euthanasia of these animals. Should a snake in your care die, a necropsy (autopsy) should be performed to determine whether a potentially communicable disease was responsible.

Experienced reptile veterinarians will also advise you on the proper housing and diet of your snakes. Healthy snakes are less likely to experience bacterial, fungal, and protozoal diseases. Proper husbandry reduces the likelihood that you, the owner, will become infected. Cage cleanliness and disinfection are critical for the maintenance of healthy snakes and the minimizing of disease transmission. Household bleach diluted to a solution of 1 to 3 ounces (about 30 to 90 milliliters) per quart (liter) of water is an excellent disinfectant that is inexpensive and widely available. This solution should be used at least once per month to clean the entire cage, once weekly to clean the water bowl, and at any time for spot cleaning. There are numerous commercial disinfectants, but they vary in effectiveness and toxicity. There is no single disinfectant that can eliminate every disease-causing organism. It is important to the health of your snake to thoroughly rinse the cage and all the cage furniture after disinfecting and before reintroducing the snake to the enclosure.

Use of the correct diet (captive-bred and captive-raised rodents or insects instead of wild-caught prey items) will tremendously reduce the risk of parasitism in snakes. Freezing your snake's food items, such as rodents and other small animals, for storage purposes has some advantages. Numerous internal and external parasites will be killed, thereby reducing the risk of human and pet snake infection. However, this technique will not kill all parasites; you should still treat these frozen and thawed food items as if they may be harboring pathogenic organisms.

As a responsible keeper, you can also reduce the risk of contracting parasites from your animals by purchasing captive-bred snakes. Though this does not entirely eliminate risks, captive-bred snakes are less likely to be heavily infested by parasites than are wild-caught snakes. Terrestrial snakes usually are not as heavily infected as aquatic snakes are, and their captive environments are less likely to harbor quite as large a variety of potentially disease-causing organisms. In general, temperate species of snakes are less heavily infested than are tropical species, although there are exceptions. Therefore, if you choose wild-caught animals, selecting species from temperate zones may reduce the risk of infestation somewhat.

The seller may have an influence on the animal's pathogenic organisms. You can reduce the risk of being infected by purchasing from a clean and reputable source. Snakes that have been housed in crowded cages at poorly managed wholesale shops and pet stores are more likely to have been exposed to these disease-causing organisms than snakes that have been purchased from private breeders and reputable stores.

Quarantine

Deal with sick animals and all newly acquired specimens with the utmost caution to avoid spreading disease to your established collection. Immediately place new arrivals in a quarantine setup; regardless of your herpetological supplier's credibility and your past experience with new snakes, a quarantine period of sixty to ninety days is recommended

for any addition to your collection. Work with your quarantined snakes only after handling your existing snakes and tools. Never move instruments, water bowls, or uneaten food items from one cage to another. Use paper towels and dispose of them after each use rather than reusing cleaning rags, which can spread pathogenic organisms if used on multiple cages.

During the quarantine period, you can observe the snakes for medical problems. Observation includes repeated fecal exams to check for internal parasites such as *Cryptosporidia* or *Entamoeba*, which could be devastating to an established collection. Eliminate all parasites (as much as possible) before allowing the snakes out of quarantine. A snake diagnosed with *Cryptosporidia* or inclusion body disease (IBD) should never be allowed into a collection.

Warn visitors to your collection of the potential risks involved, and ask them to wash their hands after handling your snakes. Do not give young children any reptile souvenirs, such as shed skins, scutes, or rattles, which could harbor *Salmonella* (Grier, Bjerke, and Nolan 1993).

Treating a Snake

Since most snakes do not vocalize or have obvious facial expressions that indicate pain, many herpetoculturists have been tempted to treat their own snakes, up to and including minor surgeries (sometimes without anesthesia). Make no mistake, snakes do feel pain. Anyone who has given an injection of an antibiotic to a ball python has seen it jump. Keep this in mind as you consider the home treatment of your pet. Most reptile-oriented veterinarians believe that oral antibiotics are generally useless in the treatment of the majority of infectious diseases of snakes. Thus, the purchase of over-the-counter oral antibiotics is not only a waste of your money but also a waste of valuable time. Over the period of time you are administering the over-the-counter product, the disease may progress and become untreatable, even with professional help. Remember this as you consider home treatment.

Injections

When administering an injection, be especially careful of a snake's sudden, violent jerks toward the needle. When we give an injection, we sometimes wrap our hands around the snake near the injection point to prevent or slow down jerking movements. Insert the needle at a slight angle, not perpendicular to the skin. If the needle is perpendicular, a sudden motion may cause it to penetrate too deeply, consequently resulting in serious harm to the snake.

The anatomy and physiology of snakes are different from that of many other animals. There are even marked differences among snake species. One difference is that snakes have a renal portal system, which basically means that all the

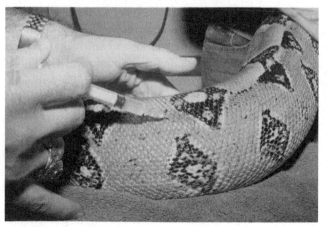

Giving a snake an injection is tricky. Snakes may jump or twist. Proper location of the injection is essential to avoid injuring the snake.

blood in the back half of the body is filtered through the kidneys before circulating to the front of the body. In other words, antibiotics should be injected into the front half of the body. Most antibiotics also should be injected intramuscularly (in the muscle). If you have never administered an injection to a snake or seen it done by a professional, you may be wasting your time, and you could injure the snake. If the injection is administered incorrectly, it may not be effectively absorbed and distributed, or it may injure the snake. Consider this possibility before you attempt home treatment. Bear in mind also that the choice of antibiotics is not an arbitrary one. Different antibiotics have different characteristics and are effective against different bacteria. In most cases, the choice should be based upon a culture and a sensitivity test. It is important to note, however, that an educated guess on the correct antibiotic must be made prior to the return of the results of the culture and sensitivity test, and that antibiotic should be administered immediately. This is a situation in which experience really counts. The antibiotic chosen can always be changed if the results show that the educated guess is incorrect.

The proper drug administered at the wrong dose is actually a poison that may cause organ damage or death. Even the proper dose when administered improperly is potentially dangerous or, at best, useless. For example, a highly irritating substance accidentally injected into the lung may cause a tremendous local reaction leading to pneumonia.

Injection of the same antibiotic subcutaneously will not be absorbed and distributed properly, thereby negating much of its effectiveness.

Thus, there are several things that need to be taken into consideration prior to attempting the treatment of your snake. Many veterinarians can now provide a great deal of assistance in diagnosing and treating snakes. (Refer to the dosage charts in chapter 16.)

Abscesses

The most common cause of a lump or bump in reptiles is an abscess, a pocket of bacteria and dead cells. The bacteria that form abscesses may invade the area via the skin or through the blood. The presence of an abscess strongly suggests that the reptile has been housed in such a manner that its immune system is not functioning properly. Therefore, the animal's housing conditions need to be corrected as part of the treatment.

If you have a strong stomach, you can treat superficial abscesses at home by incising them and flushing them with a povidone-iodine solution. Reptile pus is usually solid, not liquid, so it won't drain by itself. Manually extract the pus by applying pressure to the sides of the abscess. After you have expressed the majority of the pus, curette (scraping out the inside of the abscess with a small spoonlike instrument) the abscess.

This hognose snake has an anal gland abscess. It will require surgical drainage and antibiotics. Anal gland abscesses are most common in female snakes.

Check the snake's environment for the cause of the abscess. Is the enclosure warm enough, dry enough, clean enough? The presence of one abscess that you do see may be a warning of other abscesses you do not see. Accordingly, the treatment of abscesses almost always requires the use of systemic antibiotics following the removal of the abscesses.

Base the selection of an appropriate antibiotic upon a culture and a sensitivity test of the purulent material itself or of the inner wall of the abscess. If you drain the abscess at home, you must immediately take a sample of the pus (in a manner that precludes contamination from outside organisms) to your reptile veterinarian. One way to do this is to place a sample of the material or skin from the abscess into an inverted plastic bag without touching it with your hands. Keep in mind that the best cultures are from the

Risks Associated with At-Home Surgery

Keep in mind that there is some risk both to you and to your patient if you choose to perform minor surgical procedures on your pet snake. It is easy for an inexperienced hobbyist to confuse an abscess with mycobacterial granuloma, which is a tuberculosis-type lesion that contains bacteria contagious to humans. Additionally, if you incise what you think is an abscess but it turns out to be a tumor, you may have a bleeding mess on your hands. If this happens, apply a pressure bandage, and take the snake to a veterinarian immediately. Indeed, you may wish to consider this latter option first.

inner wall of the abscess, not the pus that is removed, so ideally it would be best to have a sterile culturette on hand and directly swab the inner wall of the abscess at the time it is opened.

If you slice open a lump and find a parasite, wash your hands immediately and take your snake to a veterinarian who has reptile experience. This is probably sparganosis (a parasitic infection in which a tapeworm becomes imbedded into the muscle or directly under the skin), and it is a more serious problem than the average snake keeper can handle because the worms are usually distributed throughout the snake, not just in the one lump.

Replicating a snake's natural environment can ameliorate some adaptation problems. This setup is appropriate for burrowing species.

Common Problems Associated with Acclimation

All animals must acclimate, that is, adjust to a changing environment. Some animals are better able to acclimate than others. This is true of snakes. Captivity may be thought of as a radically changed environment to which the snake must acclimate. Failure to acclimate well leads to a number of problems, some of which are discussed below.

Maladaptation

Maladaptation syndrome is defined as pathological effects in an animal associated with the stress of captivity (Cowan 1980). Simply stated, stress leads to disease. One example of

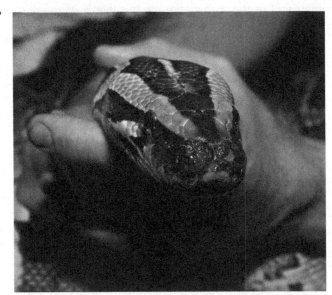

Rostral and dorsal cranial abrasions are often seen in stressed snakes kept in cages that are too small or that have inappropriate materials, such as raw wood or wire.

this syndrome is the deterioration of the pancreas in a number of rattlesnake species of genus *Crotalus* when they first arrive in captivity. Prior to medical problems, however, come behavioral signs, which indicate that something may be wrong with your snake's health. For example, snakes with maladaptation syndrome would exhibit some or all of the following: constant movement within the cage, abrasion of the nose, and failure to feed and eventual cachexia (wasting away), followed by disease and death.

About 90 percent of medical and psychological problems are either directly or indirectly related to environmental problems or husbandry practices, or both. Maladaptation syndrome may be avoided in some cases by creating an environment very similar to that from which the animal was derived. It is critical to examine the environment of a snake that exhibits any of the aforementioned behaviors and to make the best possible corrections. There are no medical miracles that will save these animals if their environments are not improved. Force-feeding is only palliative in most cases, and it is usually unnecessary if the environment has first been corrected. Multivitamin injections or metronidazole at a dose of 20 milligrams per kilogram orally will sometimes stimulate a snake to begin eating. Exactly why these latter techniques work is unknown. There are several theories that are beyond the scope of this discussion.

Overheating

As we mentioned earlier in this chapter, there's no telling how long your new snake has gone without water during transport. Overheating is a big concern, especially in hot places or during times of the year when temperatures are high. Your snake may be overheated if it moves frantically about its cage with its mouth open, especially after being exposed to direct sunlight or after being released from a transport device, such as a pillowcase. If this is the case, immediately get the snake out of the sun, and immerse it in a shallow pan of cool water (except for its head, of course). This procedure has saved many a snake. Try to avoid having to resort to this measure by using proper transportation procedures. (See the section on transporting your snake earlier in this chapter.) The presence of a large bowl of water in the cage is the snake's first line of defense if the cage gets too hot. This is one common reason snakes sit in their water bowls for long periods of time. If you see your snake doing this, check the cage temperature, using a thermometer for an accurate reading. Common causes of increased temperature are sunlight hitting the cage and a malfunctioning heating device. If

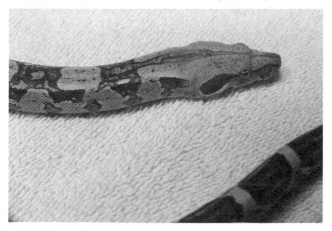

This snake exhibits signs of cerebral edema from overheating. Its head and neck are swollen, and it has signs of neurological problems.

cages are stacked, heat coming from the lighting fixture atop the lower cage may make the cage above it dangerously warm. (See chapter 2 for further discussion on enclosures, cage accessories, and controlling temperature and humidity.)

After administering the cold-water treatment, you may wish to take your snake to a reptile-oriented veterinarian for an injection of a sterile electrolyte solution and possibly for a steroid injection. We have successfully used dexamethasone at a dose of 5 milligrams per kilogram of body weight intramuscularly twice per day for small snakes on the first day after the incident. Sometimes this is all that is needed. Other veterinarians have administered 1 to 2 milligrams per kilogram once daily for two to three days (R. Klingenberg, pers. comm.) Be aware also that some snakes may be weak for days after an overheating incident; they will either recover slowly or die.

CHAPTER 2

DISEASE AND THE CAPTIVE ENVIRONMENT

P erhaps the most important concept in herpetoculture is the relationship between disease and the captive environment. If a snake is placed in a proper environment (either a natural one or a man-made re-creation of essential aspects of the natural habitat), disease is unlikely to occur. In an artificial environment, you can reduce the likelihood of disease in reptiles in the following ways: (1) cater to their immune systems by keeping them warm with access to a thermal gradient; (2) reduce stress by housing them singly and by not handling them; (3) feed them a high-quality diet; and (4) control parasites and maintain cleanliness.

With some species, however, it is essential that you re-create the natural habitat, or you will be unsuccessful in your attempt to maintain them in captivity. Examples of

Snakes living in a setup that meets their environmental needs (appropriate basking sites, shelter, and substrate) exhibit less stress and disease.

such species are crayfish snakes genus *Regina* and sand snakes genus *Chilomeniscus*. Indeed, the degree to which we perceive certain snakes as being difficult to keep in captivity is determined largely by how well they accept artificial environments and the less varied diets offered in captive situations. We regard snakes that require only a standard thermal gradient, proper humidity, simple and easy-to-replace substrate, and a hide box as easy species; snakes that require a more complex re-creation of aspects of their environments as difficult species. In both cases, the captive environment is critical, and any successful treatment of disease in reptiles will involve correcting the environment first. Cowan (1980) and Ross and Marzec (1984) provide excellent discussions on the relationship of environment and disease. (See also chapter 14 for a discussion on psychological factors that may affect your snake's ability to thrive.)

Disease-Preventing Enclosures and Procedures

It is impossible to generalize about the captive requirements of all three thousand species of snakes. The specifics are not known for most species; however, there are certain basics that are considered important in the successful maintenance of the species studied to date. These basic requirements include the following.

This naturalistic vivarium has cypress mulch. Small, secretive snakes require a substrate that provides numerous hiding places.

An outdoor enclosure can provide many benefits for a snake. However, it is vital that the cage be secure to avoid breakouts (and break-ins).

Caging

Snakes are usually most safely housed indoors in smooth-sided, well-ventilated enclosures that have a perimeter larger than the length of the snake. (Some states specify a minimum cage size that has a perimeter one and a half times the length of the snake.) Suitable caging materials include glass, plastic, and metal; these have smooth, nonporous surfaces that make them easy to disinfect. Untreated wood is generally not suitable because it is abrasive and is not easily disinfected. Treated lumber contains many toxic chemicals, which make it completely unsuitable for herpetoculture. Any enclosure used for keeping snakes should have an effective locking mechanism to prevent escape.

Substrate

The substrate (the material used on the bottom of the cage) is a critical factor in snake maintenance. The most frequently used substrates include artificial turf, newspaper, aspen shavings, pine shavings, and cypress mulch. Do not use cedar shavings, as they contain aromatic compounds that may lead to respiratory problems. (See chapter 9 for a

39

This ball python was badly abused after escaping. It was struck with a metal rod, which caused its heart to protrude. Fortunately, its heart was returned to its chest, and the snake survived.

Management of Escapes

Properly housed snakes will never escape from their cages; however, nothing in the world is perfect, and occasionally one will get away. Following is some advice on how to recapture an escapee. (This information can also be used as advice for "normal" snake-fearing people to round up an unwanted visitor from their homes without harming the snake.)

It's best to look for a lost snake at night, at least thirty minutes after all the lights in the house are turned off. Funneled minnow traps, glue boards, and piles of towels are the best trapping devices; place them where the snake was last seen. Usually, this area is in a corner or along a wall of the room in which the snake was maintained.

Minnow traps, available at your local bait store, have a narrow funneled entrance that can trap small snakes. After the snake becomes trapped in these little enclosures, you can pick up even small venomous snakes with a garden tool or a thick blanket. Once the snake is back in its cage or outside, the traps can be opened easily. To increase effectiveness, bait these traps with a dead food item.

Glue boards, such as those used to trap rodents, work well to trap escaped pet snakes and wild snakes. Nail the glue board to a piece of wood long enough to allow you to safely pick up a trapped venomous snake without being bitten. When you've moved the trapped snake to a more desirable location (your pet to its cage or a wild snake to a distant field), pour vegetable oil on the glue board to release the animal. Remove glued snakes slowly and carefully to avoid skin abrasions or lacerations.

A pile of old towels or burlap bags is an old and very successful method for capture. Keep the pile in the proper location as previously mentioned. Check it after several days to see if your missing snake has entered it. Of course, if you are suggesting this trick to someone who does not like snakes and is uncertain whether the snake being dealt with is venomous, instruct the person to use a shovel to pick up the pile of towels and carry it outside. Use the shovel to unravel the pile of towels. Once uncovered, a snake will usually flee at once, never to be seen again.

There also is the live bait option. You can place a live rodent in a bird cage or in an aquarium tank with a hole in the center of its screen top. The snake may enter the cage or aquarium to eat the rodent and become trapped until it can digest its meal. The crucial element here is the size of the hole in the screen top. It must be just large enough that a snake can pass through it with an empty stomach but not leave it with a prey bulge.

One last trick worth mentioning: if an escape occurs during cool weather, consider turning up the heat in the house. This method has been known to bring many snakes out of hiding.

Remember to thoroughly check the snake after it is recaptured. Abrasions, splinters, and lacerations may require treatment. Exotic snakes may become chilled during their wanderings and end up with respiratory infections or stomatitis (mouth rot). Antibiotics may be required.

Be a responsible snake owner and prevent escapes by utilizing appropriate and secure cages and by double-checking the lids or door regularly. Seal all holes and cracks in walls, floors, and such as soon as you become a snake owner, thereby simplifying the recapture of an escapee.

As longtime snake keepers, we are aware of the frustration of the so-called empty-cage syndrome (the fear of finding your snake has escaped). We hope these tips will aid in your recovery from this stress by helping you capture your little wanderer. Good luck!

Here are newspaper, gravel, sand (two types), mulch, and Aspen shavings, all possible choices for vivarium substrate. Depending on the species of snake, one substrate might be more appropriate than another.

discussion of common respiratory problems.) Under no circumstances should you use towels or rags, as these items hold too much moisture and can cause bacterial infections. Small snakes commonly require one of the more natural substrates, which may be mixed with soil in order to provide a semimoist burrowing medium. (See Rossi 1992 and Rossi and Rossi 1995 and 2003 for more detailed discussions on the care of small snakes.)

Shelters and Hide Boxes

Hiding places are an essential part of a well-designed enclosure. Most snake keepers provide an inverted plastic box, often called a hide box, for their snakes. It is where a well-acclimated snake will spend the majority of its time.

There are many commercial reptile products on the market that function as shelters. Products made of plastic or cork bark work extremely well because they are light and easy to clean. Some of the newer enclosure designs include a false floor (the floor has a hole in it, which leads to a large space beneath), which creates a very large, dark hiding place. Just make sure that the "floor" can be easily removed to gain access to the snake or for cleaning purposes. Examine the size of the entrance hole as well to ensure it is large enough for the snake to comfortably enter and exit.

Some herpetoculturists have discovered the benefits of situating a hide box up high in a cage; this positioning is

Hide boxes, such as the one shown here, are crucial for the psychological and physical health of snakes. There are many naturalistic models now on the market.

better accepted by some snakes, increases floor space, and provides easier accessibility for the owner at cage cleaning time. An elevated hide box is particularly well received by arboreal snakes but may also be suitable for other snakes that, like some birds, like the security of being elevated.

Humidity and Ventilation

Most snakes appear to do well if they are maintained in middle humidity ranges (between 40 and 70 percent). However, desert snakes typically require lower humidity (between 10 and 40 percent), and rain forest species require higher humidity (between 80 and 100 percent). It is important that the proper humidity be maintained but not at the expense of good ventilation. If cage ventilation is poor and the humidity is high, bacteria, mold, and fungi may grow rapidly and infect the snake. Thus, screen tops or numerous ventilation holes are necessary for most enclosures.

Temperature and the Thermal Gradient

Usually, a heat source is necessary for the normal function of a captive snake's immune system and to facilitate proper digestion. Heat is also psychologically beneficial in that it enables a snake to thermoregulate freely. Heating pads or heat tapes are necessary equipment for terrestrial captive snake maintenance. It is important to note that these heating devices need to be placed outside the cage. If you place

43

these devices inside a cage, burns and even electrocution may result. (See the section on burns in chapter 3.) Arboreal snakes may benefit from an overhead heat source, such as an incandescent bulb in a reflector-type fixture, which concentrates heat from the bulb to produce a warm spot among the branches in the cage.

You need to create a thermal gradient in the cage, providing a localized warm spot on one end of the enclosure and keeping the rest of the cage at a cooler temperature. Tropical snakes, such as boas and pythons, generally do well with a daytime temperature gradient between 80°F and 95°F (27°C and 35°C) and a nighttime gradient in which the cooler end of the cage drops no lower than 72°F (22°C) while the warm end remains in the low to mid-90s F (mid-20s C). Most temperate zone snakes will thrive with a daytime temperate gradient between 72°F and 95°F (22°C and 35°C). Keep in mind that many pet snakes are nocturnal and do not seek intense heat for any length of time. They must be able to escape it. Even the large, diurnal whip snakes and racers will not utilize the high end of their gradients for long. Nevertheless, it should be made available to them.

Some heating and cooling devices can be used in emergencies (such as to quickly cool a snake that has been accidentally overheated) or for temporary transport situations. For example, chemically activated heat packs that people

This sand boa's enclosure has a thermal gradient. The side of the cage with a heat lamp positioned over a basking rock is warm; the rest of the cage is cool.

use to soothe sore backs can be used in crates to heat snakes shipped during winter. These products are available in many drug stores and sporting goods stores. Most models produce heat for up to eight hours, but they may keep the snake warm even longer if they are being used inside of an insulated container. If there is a power outage and no other heat is available, one can also use a car's heater. However, make sure that the car is well ventilated to avoid carbon monoxide toxicity and that the plastic boxes in which the snakes are placed are well ventilated and secure.

Perhaps an emergency generator would be a good investment if you keep a large number of snakes. For long-term outages, transport your snakes to a friend's home that still has heat. Once again, make sure that the cages are secure. Nothing tests a friendship like a loose pet snake in the house!

Lighting

To date, most snakes studied in captivity appear not to require ultraviolet (UV) light. Some snakes have been maintained and bred in captivity for many years with exposure to nothing more than filtered natural light. This may or may not be supplemented with artificial light, such as that produced by fluorescent or incandescent bulbs. There is anecdotal evidence of appetite improvement in snakes exposed to full-spectrum fluorescent lights (Vita-Lite or Reptisun, for example). We strongly encourage keepers of difficult snakes to experiment with supplemental full-spectrum fluorescent and incandescent lighting to see if it will improve feeding and breeding success. Any artificial lighting should simulate a natural light cycle. Perhaps the best way to mimic the natural light cycle is to put your lights on automatic timers, set to turn the lights on at sunrise and off at sunset. This method works well for all temperate zone snakes and most tropical snakes, depending upon where you are living. Tropical snakes born in captivity will do well with this approach. Tropical snakes born in the wild and recently imported may benefit by being exposed to a light cycle similar to that where they came from, and this may require

some research. A general rule for some of these animals is to provide twelve hours of light and twelve hours of darkness most of the year, with an increase to thirteen or fourteen hours of light in the summer.

Cleaning and Disinfection

Although unnecessarily frequent (daily) cleanings may create undue stress for some snakes, the benefits of cage cleanliness seem to outweigh the risks. Spot cleaning the cage once a week is usually sufficient, but every snake is different. A water snake may defecate more frequently than a boa and thus will require more frequent cleanings. Regular cage disinfection and the removal of feces, shed skin, and uneaten food items eliminate large numbers of pathogenic bacteria and break the life cycle of metazoan parasites that have direct life cycles. In other words, cage cleanliness is important.

You should remove organic material such as feces, shed skins, and uneaten food items as soon as you notice them. A major cleaning including breakdown of the cage, removal of the substrate, scrubbing of the interior with soap, and disinfecting of the cage and all cage accessories need to be undertaken every one to three months, depending upon the species and the substrate used. A wide variety of disinfectants have been recommended for use with reptiles. We think the most economical and effective disinfectant available is household bleach. Other disinfectants may have a broader spectrum of activity, but generally they are very toxic, are quite expensive, are not readily available, or have an inadequate shelf life. For these reasons, we strongly recommend bleach as a standard disinfectant. An effective dilution rate is 1 to 3 ounces of bleach (30 to 90 milliliters) per quart (liter) of water. This solution should be used at least once per month in the cage and once weekly to clean the water bowl. It may also be used for spot cleaning each time an animal defecates. (A more detailed discussion of disinfectants is presented in Rossi and Rossi 2003.)

CHAPTER 3

SKIN

S kin is the largest organ of the body. It is perhaps one of the most important as well because it serves to protect organisms from their environment. In reptiles, problems of the skin are often the first signs of a failure to provide the proper environment; if left untreated, skin problems will often lead to a snake's demise. Skin problems also may signal a major internal problem, so it is imperative to seek help from a reptile-oriented veterinarian if the afflicted snake's condition doesn't improve after correcting the environment.

Burns

Thermal burns are among the most common problems of captive snakes. In many cases, these injuries can be avoided if you exercise common sense and regularly observe the snakes in your care. Treatment is possible, but often it is a prolonged and painful experience for the snake, with permanent scarring a typical outcome. Additionally, lengthy treatment will be an expensive ordeal for the owner. The

This snake has unshed skin, which may be caused by an improper environment in its vivarium. Keeping your snake's skin healthy is primarily a matter of environmental management.

Burns such as this one are usually caused by improper use of heat lamps or other heating devices, such as hot rocks and heat tape.

goal of this section is to teach snake keepers how to prevent burns from occurring and how to treat burns if they do. (See also the following section on dermatitis.)

Prevention

Burns can usually be prevented by following several simple rules.

1. Do not place any heating device (heating pads, heat tapes, and even lights) inside the cage or anywhere that the snake can come into direct contact with it. Because hot rocks are incriminated in many burn cases, we do not recommend them. Do not assume that the snake will avoid contact with something that is very hot, such as a lightbulb. Following this rule will also prevent your snake from accidentally electrocuting itself if it spills its water bowl.

2. Do not heat the entire floor or entire top of a cage. Heating only a portion of the enclosure will allow the snake to select cool areas according to its needs, as part of the natural process of thermoregulation.

3. Do not place the snake's cage in direct sunlight, especially if it is a glass cage, which can have an oven effect that will very quickly overheat your snake, possibly killing the animal.

4. Make sure that the cage is well ventilated. Ventilation allows excess heat to rise and escape the enclosure, thereby affording the snake extra protection from overheating.

Never allow a snake to come into direct contact with a heat lamp or any other heating device.

5. Use a thermometer for an accurate reading of the cage temperature.
6. Check your heating devices regularly by feeling the heated areas to be sure the devices are working properly. (Still monitor the overall cage temperature with a thermometer.)
7. Replace heating devices regularly. Many appear to become progressively hotter after two years of continuous usage.

Treatment

Treatment of burns is much more difficult than their prevention. The first step in treating any burn is to remove whatever caused the burn. Do not, however, remove the snake's heat source altogether. If you have to remove a heating device, such as an overhead heat lamp, have a replacement ready to install or an alternative, temporary heat source. Providing less than adequate heat will compromise the snake's immune response just when it may be needed most. Use a dependable, gentle heat source such as a high-quality heating pad turned on low and placed outside of the cage, as part of the treatment regime. In addition, you should use an insulating substrate such as indoor/outdoor carpet, which will not allow the snake to nestle it out of the way to sit on the hot cage bottom.

The second step is to apply topical antibiotic ointment (such as Polysporin, Silvadene Cream 1%, or Betadine) to the lesions once daily for a period of three to four weeks. In many cases, it is advisable to allow the snake to soak in a povidone-iodine solution for thirty minutes per day prior to applying the ointment.

In severe cases, which most burns are, injectable antibiotics are necessary to prevent secondary bacterial infections and will help the snake recover. (See the following section on dermatitis as well as the dosage charts in chapter 16.) Your reptile veterinarian will probably recommend that the skin lesions be cultured in order to determine which antibiotic is the best one to use. Depending upon the severity of the burn, it may require two to four weeks of an injectable antibiotic along with topical treatment of one of the aforementioned medications for four to eight weeks.

Burns heal slowly. Extensive burns commonly require numerous ecdyses (sheddings) to heal. Burned areas may slough the epidermal layer completely and expose raw, seeping tissue. These areas will decrease in size with each shedding until they are completely healed. Scarring is the norm, leaving a permanent reminder of the incident.

A heat lamp that was too hot caused the hyperpigmentation in this snake. Always use a thermometer to ensure all lights are safe.

Dermatitis (Skin Lesions)

Burns, bite wounds, abrasions, retained skin from an attempted shed, skin tumors, parasites, excessive moisture of the substrate or high humidity, and filthy cages all may predispose snakes to dermatitis (an infection of the skin) by allowing the entry of bacteria. Since most skin lesions in snakes are occupied by bacteria, rather than caused by them, veterinarians regard lesions as secondary infections and look for causes among those listed above. Once the bacteria are established, they become a major factor in the course of the disease and must be treated to save the infected animal. Without antibiotics in the bloodstream (usually administered to reptiles by injection), bacteria may spread rapidly, causing abscesses, stomatitis (mouth rot), pneumonia, cellulitis (infection into deeper tissues, causing a swollen appearance of an area), septicemia (bacteria in the bloodstream), and death. The antibiotics chosen should be based upon a culture and sensitivity test. Ideally, the primary cause should be determined and eliminated.

Dermatitis may also be caused by mites, fungi, worms, or a viral invader. (A virus has not yet been isolated from skin lesions in snakes, although there are several in other groups of reptiles.) Worms and mites may be treated with the appropriate antiparasitic agent (see chapter 5). Suspected tumors need to be surgically removed. Retained shed skin or other factors contributing to the dermatitis should be elimi-

This snake died of septicemia, which likely started as a severe case of dermatitis.

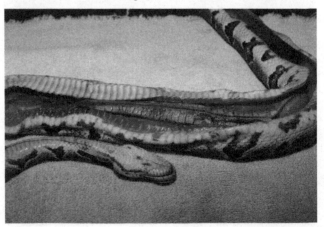

This water snake has severe fungal dermatitis. Although the snake recovered with medication and a move to a dry, warm environment, it was left partially blinded.

nated. Fungal lesions and fungal infections will respond to warmth, dryness, and daily applications of a povidone-iodine ointment, such as Betadine, or in combination with one of many antifungal ointments, including Tinactin, Micatin, and Veltrim. We have also had limited success with a diluted extract of melaleuca, and this may be worth looking into more thoroughly. Although Nystatin and Fulvicin have been tried, we have not yet found systemic antifungal agents used in mammals and other reptiles to work well on the external fungal lesions of snakes.

Fungal and bacterial infections alike may take more than a month of daily topical treatment applications to heal. Generally, we put the snake into a container in which we have placed paper towels soaked in diluted Betadine solution and leave the animal there for thirty to sixty minutes. We then remove the snake, rinse it off, and apply the antifungal ointment to its lesions. Betadine works well when it is diluted with water at a ratio of 1 part Betadine to 4 parts water.

Infections that are primarily bacterial have responded well to the Betadine bath treatment alone or to the bath followed by antibacterial topical treatments. In some cases, topicals work well even when used alone. Silvadene Cream 1% is an excellent topical for reptiles (Rosskopf 1992); it has become very popular. Polysporin ointment also works well. As with any infection in snakes, supplemental heat is a good

idea; remember that it will increase evaporation, so the snake must have access to water at all times. The use of artificial turf is therapeutic for many skin lesions because it allows fresh air to circulate under the snake. We have seen many minor lesions heal without any antibiotics when snakes have been housed on clean, dry artificial turf.

If you see no improvement in response to environmental correction and topical medications, consult a veterinarian to diagnose the specific cause of the skin lesions. The veterinarian may choose to perform a biopsy and culture and sensitivity tests to determine the best way to cure the skin problem and to determine which antibiotic is best for the infection. (See Jacobson 1988 and 1991 or Rossi 1996 for more detailed discussions on reptile dermatology.)

Dysecdysis (Improper Shedding)

Most captive snakes shed every one to three months, preceded by a blueing or clouding of the skin and eyes, which then partially return to normal just prior to the actual shed. Healthy snakes, when maintained properly, will usually shed their skins in one piece. Normal shedding is called ecdysis. Difficult shedding (that is, when the shed skin comes off in many pieces) is referred to as dysecdysis and may be caused by parasites, malnutrition, infection, metabolic irregularities, or tumors. The most common reason for dysecdysis, though, is poor environment—the relative humidity is too low, the substrate is too drying, there is no slightly rough surface to rub against, and so on. Most shedding problems can be corrected by adjusting the environment.

If a snake needs help immediately, place it in a pillowcase dampened with warm water. (Don't forget to tie the top!) Do not place the pillowcase anywhere that water could overflow and cover the bag, such as in a sink or a tub with a slow drip, and do not place the pillowcase where the snake can fall or get stepped on. A good safe place to put the snake is on the floor of a small closet. Remove the snake after thirty to sixty minutes. If the snake is truly ready to shed, the skin will be loose and easily removed with little effort. Assist with shedding by gently removing all of its old skin including the eye caps, or spectacles. If the eye caps do not come off with the shed skin, use a wet cotton-tipped applicator to remove them. Use the applicator to apply a gentle pressure in a circular motion for about fifteen minutes. If you don't succeed during this time, quit and repeat the whole process again in a few days, or take the snake to a reptile-oriented veterinarian. If you force a spectacle off prematurely, you could expose the cornea, and the snake could lose the eye.

Some over-the-counter products sold to help snakes shed are no more than expensive soap mixtures. That is not to say that they do not help; they do, by helping water enter the old skin. You can achieve the same effect by using a couple of drops of mild dishwashing detergent in the soaking

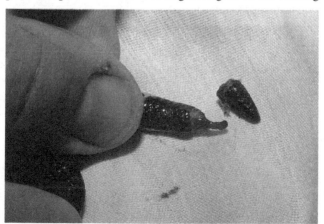

During its shed, this snake retained skin at the tip of its tail, causing blood constriction and, later, tail loss. If shedding problems don't resolve with an environment change, see your veterinarian.

A rat, left overnight in the cage, chewed up this snake. Never leave live food with a snake. Better yet, only feed prekilled rodents to a snake.

process described above. A dilute solution of one part hydrogen peroxide to three or four parts water has also been found to help snakes shed more easily.

Trauma (Rodent Injuries, Escape Injuries)

Skin trauma is among the most common reasons that snakes are brought to veterinarians for treatment. The majority of these injuries fall into three major categories. The first and most common category is bite wounds, which occur when live rodents are left unattended in a snake's cage. The second category comprises injuries received by animals that escape; these are scratches, abrasions, splinters, and burns. The third category involves the usually willful injury that occurs when an escaped snake is found by a neighbor who is unappreciative of snakes.

Most bite injuries will become infected without medical treatment. Even if the wound is small, take your snake to the veterinarian.

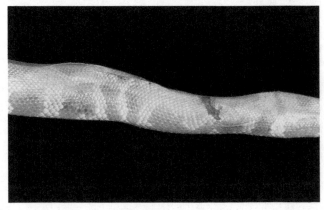

All three types of injuries may be severe or even fatal. Yet they are all preventable! Never leave a live rodent unattended in a snake's cage. Feeding prekilled rodents only is an excellent way to prevent injury to your snake. Frozen rodents are now widely available and are economical. The use of secure cages will prevent the other two types of injuries. Neodesha reptile cages are virtually escape proof. They consist of a molded one-piece body and a tight-fitting, sliding front door. Their lack of sharp corners and abrasive materials reduces the likelihood of trauma within the cage.

Once an injury has occurred, you must evaluate the severity to determine the proper treatment. Almost all bite wounds and other open wounds are likely to become

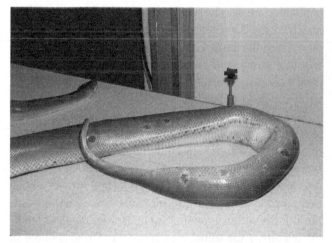

This albino green python's back was broken when it was caught under a door. The snake had to be euthanized.

infected. As with treating dermatitis, topical ointments are usually effective for treating skin trauma, but systemic (injectable) antibiotics are often necessary as well. The ointment you choose should be placed on the wound once per day. It may take several months to heal completely. Of course, any inadequacies in the environment and the diet of these animals need to be corrected, or all treatments will fail. Heavy feeding is advisable during this time to increase healing and to improve the immune response.

Crushing injuries, such as those caused when a cage lid falls on a snake or when a snake is run over by a vehicle, may respond to immediate fluids injected into the injured area.

Not only do such injections immediately restore the shape to the damaged area, but they also improve circulation. We have seen snakes with severe injuries survive after being treated in this manner. Systemic (and sometimes oral) antibiotics are also warranted in these cases because there may be some damage to the gut. We recommend that you do not feed the injured animal for several weeks following a crushing injury, and then only very small meals. A large meal may cause more trauma, possibly even reopening a small tear that was healing.

Skeletal or spinal injuries may also be present and can be severe. In many instances (both in the wild and in captivity), these will heal without any kind of treatment. In some cases, however, it may be necessary to repair the damage. Most veterinarians will need to radiograph (x-ray) such an animal to determine what kind of repair may be necessary or possible. Injuries of this type may even result in paralysis below the fracture if the spinal cord is severed. Snakes injured in this manner may survive and heal to some extent, even eventually developing a "spinal crawl," a reflex crawling that assists in locomotion. However, these snakes are unlikely candidates for breeding.

Open wounds will usually heal by scarring over. A veterinarian may reduce this effect by suturing (applying stitches to) a clean, fresh wound. This needs to be done within several hours of the trauma taking place. If more time elapses, most veterinarians will consider the wound too contaminated to attempt closing it. Bite wounds are considered contaminated immediately, and most veterinarians will not close such a wound.

CHAPTER 4

STOMATITIS

nfections of the mouth are very common in snakes. Always examine a snake's mouth before purchasing it and as part of a routine examination to ascertain a snake's health. Abnormal closure of the mouth is the first clue that something is not right. Small red spots of hemorrhage (formally, petechiations) is another indicator of possible infection. These two signs may also occur immediately after a big meal, so this is not always the best time to examine a snake. (On a side note, regurgitation following a large meal is another reason to avoid handling a snake for examination soon after it has eaten.)

More definitive signs of infection are swelling, discoloration of the mouth, and a cheeselike matter along the gum line. Advanced stomatitis (mouth rot) may be accompanied by excessive mucus in the mouth; most likely this is a result of fluid coming from the trachea, which could indicate pneumonia. Should the exudates be firmly attached to the lining of the mouth, it probably indicates membranous or diphtheritic stomatitis, which is the most severe form of stomatitis and usually extremely difficult to cure.

Always examine a snake's mouth before purchase. A normal snake mouth is pale pink and free of red spots, crust, and excessive mucus.

Untreated, even mild stomatitis can become severe within a period of days. As with all other kinds of infections, the first step in treating stomatitis is correcting the environment and supplementing the heat. After that, appropriate antibiotic therapy based upon a culture and a sensitivity test is advisable. Gram-negative bacteria are most likely responsible, and antibiotics effective against gram-negative bacteria are the most logical choice of medication.

In addition to injectable antibiotic therapy, topical medication of the mouth is usually necessary. Topical povidone-iodine solution works well in most cases, and hydrogen peroxide has also been useful. Some veterinarians combine these two products, believing that the hydrogen peroxide will help drive the povidone-iodine (Betadine) deeper into tissues, thereby making it more effective. Another topical that we have used with a great deal of success is Gentocin Ophthalmic Solution (Schering-Plough). Numerous other topical solutions have been tried with varying degrees of success, but in our experience, these three, or combinations of them, work very well.

Recently, chlorhexidine (Nolvasan 2%, nonscented solution) diluted water (1 part chlorhexidine to 20 to 30 parts water) has been used with excellent results as a topical for stomatitis. Suedemeyer (1992) stated that this solution is commonly effective against many strains of pseudomonas (bacteria). He suggests the inclusion of chlorhexidine discs on cultures and sensitivity tests. To administer any solution, gently open the mouth and remove any dead tissues. Then place several drops of the solution on the top and the bottom of the snake's mouth once or twice per day, depending upon the severity of the stomatitis. We gently restrain the snake, open the mouth with a blunt probe, and gently scrape out the material with a scalpel (#15 blade).

CHAPTER 5

PARASITES

Parasites are the bane of snake keepers. They are ubiquitous and devastating. If you keep snakes, you must maintain a constant vigil against both internal and external parasites. Have fecal exams performed annually and perhaps two or three times the first year after you acquire the snake. Observe your snakes daily for signs of external parasites, and exercise caution when bringing in food, caging material, and especially other snakes! Do it for them, and do it for yourself! Quarantine, quarantine, and in case you didn't understand, quarantine! How long? Generally speaking, as long as you can stand it. The general recommended quarantine period is two to three months, but a longer period would be even better.

External Parasites

External parasites, most notably mites and ticks, can cause shedding problems, consume blood and cellular fluids, and possibly contribute to the spread of bacterial infections. Mites are also suspected of transmitting fungal, viral, and

Left untreated, a severe mite infestation can lead to dehydration, starvation, and ultimately death, as in the case of this snake.

A mite may have either penetrated into sensitive tissues behind the eye of this snake or allowed a bacterial infection to get started there, causing the snake's head to tilt.

blood parasite infections, but there is presently little evidence for this. Until studies confirm that mites are not vectors, it is wise to assume they are. Make every effort to keep mites out of your collection and eliminate them if detected.

Snake mites (*Ophionyssus natricis*) appear to the naked eye as small black beetles. Young mites and eggs are barely visible as small white specks. Generally, mites are usually seen in the water bowl because numerous adult mites drown there. Mites tend to congregate around a snake's eyes, where they cause periorbital swelling and a sunken-eye appearance. A wet cotton swab run around the rim of the eye will often collect several mites, which can be placed under a microscope to confirm the diagnosis. Alternately, you can apply eye ointment around the eyes, and mites will evacuate or suffocate.

New snakes are the main cause of mite outbreaks. All new snakes should be quarantined for two to three months and examined regularly during this time for the presence of mites. Quarantine protects an established collection from these pests, which can spread rapidly from cage to cage.

Food items, even domestic mice raised in enclosures, are commonly a source of mites or other infectious organisms. For this reason, the purchase of "clean" mice is also an important factor in parasite control. Controlling parasites is even more difficult if you are maintaining a snake that you are feeding nondomestic food items, such as wild-caught

lizards, snakes, birds, or other prey. Freezing these items help to reduce the possibility of a mite infestation, but it doesn't eliminate the risk.

Parasites can be treated at home, but remember that your veterinarian may be able to assist you tremendously in eliminating these pests. You may want to consult him or her immediately if you have a severe infestation of one specimen or if you have a large collection at risk.

The Soaking Method

If the outbreak is not too severe, you can usually attempt treatment and control of the parasites yourself. The snake itself may try to drown numerous parasites by soaking in the water dish for days on end. This behavior should alert you to the possibility of mites. The problem with the snake's attempt is that many of the mites will escape by migrating to the snake's head, which it must keep out of water to breathe. The standard home treatment for mites makes use of this natural behavior: soak the snake in soapy water (a few drops of dish soap in a liter of water should be sufficient) and paint its head with olive oil or corn oil (not petroleum-based oils, which may be toxic or irritating). While the snake is soaking, thoroughly disinfect the cage. Dilute sodium hypochlorite solution (bleach at a concentration of 1 to 3 ounces per quart, 30 to 60 mL per liter, of water) works well as a cage disinfectant.

Sevin Dust

Sevin dust (5 percent) has proven to be an extremely effective way to eliminate mites, both in cages and on snakes, even though the safety of this method is a concern to some veterinarians because overexposure to this product can be dangerous. Use as described below, and there should be few problems. After cleaning and rinsing the cage, Levell (1992) advises sprinkling the powder into the cage (up to 1/8 inch, 3 mm, deep), letting it sit for several hours, and even placing the snake in with the powder for 24 hours. Mites are eliminated, and most snakes appear unharmed. Then rinse and dry both the cage and snake. Repeat the treatment two weeks later. Be aware that Sevin dust treatment may be tricky, however, particularly if the snake is in shed at the time of treatment. We would advise a more limited exposure, perhaps only a "shake and bake" approach: Place the dust and the snake into a pillowcase. Keep the snake inside the bag for about an hour (don't shake it!). Then rinse the snake, dry it off, and place it into a disinfected cage as described above.

Powders and Sprays

Avoid most mammalian flea powders or sprays; many of these organophosphate-based insecticides are toxic to reptiles. Even Sevin dust can be toxic if not used judiciously.

A spray that recently has been recommended by reptile-oriented veterinarians is a mixture of ivermectin and water, at a rate of a half-milliliter of Ivomec per quart (liter) of water (Abrahams 1992). It doesn't mix well, so shake regularly before each use, and discard the solution after one month. We recommend spraying the solution directly onto the snake as well as the inside and outside of the cage and cage accessories every three days for at least three weeks. Others advise that treatment for up to eight weeks may be necessary (DeNardo and Wozniak 1997).

Your veterinarian can also administer an injection of ivermectin (Ivomec) at a dose of 0.2 milligrams per kilogram of body weight (equals roughly 0.1 milligram per pound of snake, which is 0.01 cubic centimeters per pound

[0.01 mL/lb] of snake if using the undiluted 10 milligram per milliliter solution). The injected solution will usually kill all of the mites and ticks as well as many of the internal parasites with only two doses given two weeks apart. However, Roger Klingenberg, a very well-respected reptile parasitologist and veterinarian, cautions that injectable ivermectin in snakes is not without risk; he warns that neurological side effects are more likely to occur with an injection than with the spray (pers. comm.).

This snake was poisoned by an insecticide in an attempt to rid it of mites. If your snake shows signs of toxicity after being treated for external parasites, immediately wash the snake with soap and water and see a veterinarian.

Cage Cleaning

It is imperative to clean the cage regardless of what parasite treatment method you use. One of the most important parts of eliminating parasites with direct life cycles is environmental control (Klingenberg 2005). If you can't thoroughly disinfect cage furniture (a large piece of porous wood, for example), throw it away and replace it. Temporarily simplify the cage environment by using newspaper as a substrate, which will need to be replaced every two to three days. Remember that anything brought in from outside must be completely disinfected. In fact, failure to do so may have been the reason for the initial outbreak of mites.

Untreated wooden cages with many cracks and crevices are notoriously difficult to rid of mites. You'd probably have to paint the cage to seal the crevices or replace the entire cage. Soak all items in the cage in a bleach solution (1 ounce of bleach per quart, 30mL per liter of water), or bake them at 350° F (177° C) for fifteen minutes to kill off bacteria and parasites. Or, throw the cage accessories away and replace them with new, disinfected items. In some cases, these measures must be taken for all of the cages in the same room; at least for all cages adjacent to those that are infested with mites. In many cases, the treatment of the cage with 5 percent Sevin dust and a follow-up treatment two weeks later are helpful. We also recommend sprinkling Sevin dust onto the floor of a snake room, around the base of the cages, to help prevent parasites from spreading from cage to cage.

One alternative is to place a piece of a Vapona-laden strip (such as a No-Pest Strip) in the cage. We have used 1 inch (2.5 cm) of the strip for each 10 gallons (38 liters) of tank space. Place the strip directly on top of the screen lid. You can also put the strip into a small container (such as a film container into which you have punched holes), and place it directly into the cage. The recommended method is to use the strip in or on the cage for three hours every three days (remove the water during the time that the strip is over the cage). After three hours, remove the strip, and put the water back into the cage. Theoretically, the method should be used for a period of eight weeks. However, we have had success eliminating mites after treating for only three weeks. After the treatment period is over, wrap the strip in a plastic bag and save it for future use; when stored properly, the strips maintain effectiveness for several years.

Warnings About the Use of Vapona

There has been some question as to the efficacy of Vapona-laden strips. It appears that some mites may be developing a resistance to the active ingredient (Todd 1983; Peterson and Orr 1990). In addition, the safety of this product for some snakes has been questioned. Levell (1992) suggests that some members of the genus *Thamnophis* (garter snakes) appear to develop a "temporary paralysis," although Mader and DeRemer (1992) indicate that some pythons may show severe neurological signs when exposed to this insecticide. Indeed, we have noticed some degree of lethargy in garter snakes (genus *Thamnophis*) and water snakes (genus *Nerodia*) exposed to Vapona, but we have never had any fatalities and still regard it as a fairly effective and safe product if used properly.

A ball python that had been in captivity for two years passed these large tapeworms. To prevent such problems, snakes must receive regular fecal exams during their first year in captivity.

Internal Parasites

Like most other animals, snakes may have internal parasites, such as worms, that they typically acquire by ingesting food items that act as intermediate hosts. Some parasites enter the snake's body by penetrating its skin, whereas others are ingested with substrate in infrequently cleaned cages. Snakes also can be infected by protozoan parasites. With early detection, most of the worms and many of the protozoan pests are treatable.

Snakes get similar kinds of worms as dogs and cats contract in terms of the kinds of damage these parasites do, their longevity, and the appearance of their eggs. These are hookworms, roundworms, whipworms, and tapeworms. Thus, it is not surprising to find that many of these worms respond to the same medications that are used for treating canines and felines: fenbendazole (Panacur), ivermectin (Ivomec), and praziquantel (Droncit), among others. Ivermectin will kill some ophidian roundworms, whipworms, and hookworms; praziquantel will kill tapeworms and trematodes (flukes). Fenbendazole is an extremely useful and safe agent for eliminating roundworms, whipworms, hookworms, and many tapeworms. It appears to be more effective than ivermectin in eliminating worms that are commonly found in ball pythons (Klingenberg 1992). We have found it especially useful in small snakes, in which cases ivermectin can be very dangerous, or in very heavily parasitized snakes, such as those that have recently been captured, in which using ivermectin can be risky. We will often treat the snakes with fenbendazole first and follow up with ivermectin later.

The most common protozoan parasites to infect snakes are amoeba and coccidia. Amoeba can be treated with metronidazole (Flagyl), whereas coccidia can be treated with sulfadimethoxine (Albon, Bactrovet). (See the dosage charts in chapter 16.) Although you should make every effort to identify the parasites present by microscopic examination of the feces before treating the snakes, it is not a bad idea to combine a routine deworming of new snakes with a quarantine period before admitting them into a room with an established collection.

The routine deworming should include the use of both ivermectin and praziquantel for snakes that are likely to have tapeworms, including those species of snakes that consume fish, amphibians, or other reptiles—such as hognose snakes (genus *Heterodon*), indigo snakes (genus

This snake has amoebiasis, an infection of the colon that can be indicated by bloody diarrhea.

Drymarchon), kingsnakes (genus *Lampropeltis*), coral snakes (genus *Micrurus*), and cobras (family Elapidae).

Fenbendazole alone is a suitable substance for routine deworming, but it will probably not get all of the tapeworms, so you may want to reserve it for mild cases or for very small snakes. If you want to be sure you've eliminated the worms, bring a fecal sample to a reptile-oriented veterinarian and ask him or her to do a worm check for you. Any worms can be identified (at least by a major category), and protozoa may be detected. The veterinarian can then either advise you on what medications

Administering deworming agents to a very large snake is a job for at least two people—and often requires more.

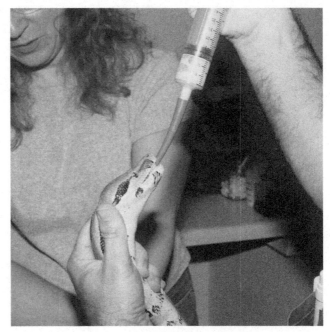

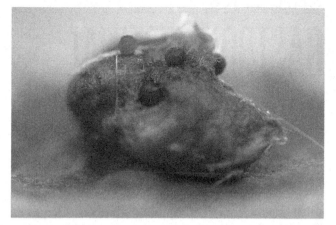

The small orange spheres in this rattlesnake fecal sample are tapeworm segments. Look for signs of internal parasites in feces.

to use and their correct doses or treat your snake properly and safely for you. Most veterinarians will recommend that the snake be examined and carefully weighed before dispensing or administering any medications. This is the way it should be done in most cases.

CHAPTER 6

GASTROINTESTINAL PROBLEMS

astrointestinal problems are extremely common in captive snakes. These problems include constipation, diarrhea, vomiting, and regurgitation. Veterinarians refer to these problems as signs and look for an underlying cause. In many instances, the cause is directly or indirectly related to an improper environment—that is, not enough heat, too much humidity, or other problematic situations. In these cases, a parasite or an opportunistic microorganism can gain a foothold. Hence, the treatment of all gastrointestinal problems must involve an evaluation and correction of the environment as well as elimination of the bacteria, fungi, or worms.

Diarrhea

Diarrhea is the occurrence of loose, watery, and usually foul-smelling stools. The causes of diarrhea in snakes are similar

This snake is over-heated—one of the more unusual causes of diarrhea in snakes. Diarrhea is often resolved when the temperature is raised or lowered.

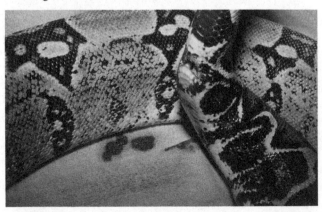

to causes of vomiting—infection, stress, or feeding irregularity, to name a few. In many cases, both signs (diarrhea and vomiting) occur when a snake is unhealthy. As with vomiting (and indeed with most other medical problems in snakes), the first part of the treatment for diarrhea is to correct the environment. One should especially try increasing the heat in the cage first. Diarrhea will sometimes respond to increased environmental temperature alone. If the problem persists, you must seek medical treatment. Repeated fecal exams or a gastric wash may reveal protozoan, fungal, or metazoan parasites, and a fecal culture and sensitivity test may reveal primary or secondary bacterial invaders causing the loose stools. Once the nature of the guilty organism is

Examine your snake's stools regularly. Are they loose or dry? Call your veterinarian if you notice anything unusual.

determined, it may be eliminated with an appropriate parasiticide, antifungal agent, or antibiotic. A veterinarian may also replace fluid losses and provide supportive care. However, do not delay medical treatment too long or it may become a very serious, if not fatal, problem. Frye (1991) advises the use of Kaopectate at a dose directly related to the weight of the snake. We have successfully used a dose of 1 milliliter per kilogram of body weight on small snakes. Only one dose was needed in our particular situation, but you may wish to administer it once daily for two or three days. If diarrhea persists longer than that, stop and seek veterinary attention. Do not handle the snake except as is necessary to treat the animal until after the diarrhea stops. (See also the section on dehydration in chapter 7.)

Remember that loose, foul-smelling stools may be normal for any snake being fed a diet primarily of fish or amphibians. Less odorous and firmer stools may form immediately after switching the snake's diet to scented mice.

Constipation

Overfed, underactive snakes are prime candidates for constipation. Some snakes that are fed frozen and thawed food items tend to become dehydrated as a consequence of fluid loss in prey items during the freeze thaw cycle. Other factors that can contribute to constipation are cooler temperatures and lower humidity than the snake is used to. Cooler air temperatures can cause a snake to "hug" its heat source; by doing so, the inactive snake essentially "cooks" the stool in its colon for several days, thereby drying it out and making it more difficult to pass. Lower cage humidity increases the rate of evaporative water loss even more and worsens an already serious situation. Without any intervention, the snake's stools may become as hard as rocks, which is why they are called fecoliths (fecal stones). Chronic constipation (formally, obstipation, noted by hard stools every three to five days) may result in quite a backup, especially as many snakes continue eating even when constipated.

There are a number of treatments for constipation. The first and most important action is to correct the environment. Eliminate drying substrates, such as corncob litter. Wood and cardboard fixtures are also very drying and thus should be removed from the cage. Avoid using cages with sides made of untreated wood as these types may also dry out the air within the cage. Other treatment options to consider include using a humidifier, increasing the size of the cage and providing additional accessories to encourage exercise, or reducing the frequency of feeding or feeding smaller and more digestible items. Renowned reptile veterinarian Steven Divers (pers. comm.) suggests that injecting water into frozen and thawed prey items may be helpful.

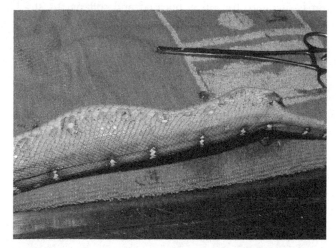

The next step in treating constipation is to try several warm water soaks. Placing the snake in shallow, warm water for fifteen minutes per day for three or four days will usually cause it to defecate. If not, an enema of warm water or of a very dilute solution of dioctyl sodium sulfosuccinate (DSS) will likely work. Frye (1991) quotes Paul-Murphy and colleagues (1987) in advising that DSS be diluted at a ratio of one part DSS (standard stock solution) to 20 parts water if the solution is to be administered through a stomach tube. Frye also advises the use of magnesium oxide (milk of magnesia) suspension or mineral oil in small amounts as aids for constipation. One mL/kg of body weight is a safe dose for milk of magnesia.

A small quantity of mineral oil (1 mL/kg of body weight) administered through a stomach tube has long been recommended and, indeed, does seem to work. However, the administration must be made by someone experienced in tubing reptiles as the improper placement may lead to regurgitation as well as aspiration of the oil and result in pneumonia. One means of administering the mineral oil that we have found successful has been jokingly referred to by the senior author as "mouse lax" or "rat lax." Basically, if a snake is still feeding, you can offer a prekilled mouse or rat that has been injected with the appropriate dose of mineral oil. Several days later, when the mouse or

75

rat is digested, the oil is released and softens the stool; defecation occurs within several days to a few weeks.

If the above approach proves unsuccessful, surgical removal of the fecoliths is necessary. However, the best approach to this problem is prevention. Avoid overfeeding your snake, provide it with as much room as possible, and maintain appropriate temperature and humidity ranges. Although some sources have suggested that routine handling may be good exercise for the snake, remember that some animals do not tolerate handling very well.

There are many reasons a snake may regurgitate or vomit, including an environmental temperature that is too low, a sudden change in temperature in either direction, and being handled too soon after eating.

Vomiting and Regurgitation

Another common reason that snakes are brought to veterinarians for exams is that they are regurgitating or vomiting. Regurgitation occurs soon after eating, whereas vomiting occurs hours or days after ingestion of food. Regurgitated food is generally undigested food expelled primarily from the esophagus (passively, that is, without much force). Vomitus consists of partially digested food, usually actively expelled from the stomach. With reptiles, distinguishing between the two actions can sometimes be difficult. The point is that the snake is not holding down food, and possible causes are numerous.

There are ten common causes for vomiting or regurgitation in snakes, but remember that there may be more than one cause for any particular case. A good example of this has been termed "regurgitation syndrome" by Ross and Marzec (1990), which occurs in all snakes, although Ross and Marzec were studying boid snakes at the time the phrase was coined. Following are the ten common causes for vomiting or regurgitation in snakes:

1. Handling too much or too soon after feeding
2. A sharp (sudden) drop or rise in ambient temperature or just improper ambient temperature for digestion
3. Increased stress (including from mating) soon after feeding
4. A meal that is too large, too old, or too toxic or offered too frequently
5. Bacterial infection
6. Protozoal infection (amoeba, coccidian, flagellate)
7. Metazoan (worm) infection
8. Tumor
9. Excessive drinking right after eating
10. Dehydration

Sometimes, making minor changes to a snake's environment or adding a new animal to the enclosure may be very stressful for the snake and cause it to vomit its last meal. Perhaps the most common cause of vomiting or regurgitation is an ambient temperature that does not allow normal digestion. More frequently, a drop in ambient temperature is the cause of sudden onsets of vomiting or regurgitation, yet it also can be caused by sharp rises in temperature. This symptom should serve as a warning to the herpetoculturist that the normal ambient temperature may be marginal for digestion.

Very large meals may cause irritation of the gastrointestinal tract and may result in vomiting or regurgitation. Too-frequent feedings have the same effect. In snakes, irritation

Handling After Feeding

Handling a snake right after it has fed is asking for trouble. Wait at least two days, depending upon the size of the meal.

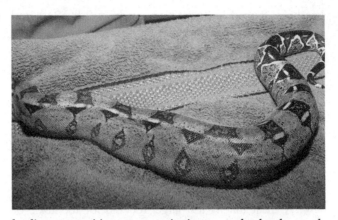

leading to vomiting or regurgitation may also be the result of swallowing a large meal backward; the scales of a fish or the fur of a mammal—which generally are directed from nose to tail—would be pushed up if the prey were swallowed tail end first and would irritate the snake's insides. If the prey offered has been in freezer storage for a long time, perhaps longer than six months, it may be loaded with bacteria or bacterial toxins, which in some cases may induce vomiting or regurgitation as happens with humans in cases of food poisoning. Some food items, such as certain species of frogs and toads, produce chemical toxins that may be a little more than some snakes can handle.

Bacteria flourish in a filthy environment. Bacteria that are extremely contagious are commonly discovered as the cause of outbreaks of vomiting. These bacteria may be responsible for an inflammation of the lining of the stomach and intestine known as bacterial gastroenteritis. Not surprisingly, two of the contagious gram-negative bacteria, *Salmonella* and *Arizona*, are frequent offenders. These bacterial infections are among the few cases in snake medicine in which oral antibiotics are deemed appropriate and necessary. Ross and Marzec (1984) and Ross and Marzec (1990) have used ciprofloxacin and amoxicillin successfully. The senior author of this book commonly uses ciprofloxacin and enrofloxacin orally in snakes with gastroenteritis, at the doses listed in the drug tables at the back of the book, and it has worked very well.

Since we discuss parasites (protozoan and metazoan) in some detail in the last chapter, we will not dwell upon them here. However, you should always consult your veterinarian if you suspect parasites. It is usually a waste of time and money—not to mention dangerous for the snake—to pump one routine deworming agent after another into a debilitated snake without the benefit of repeated fecal exams or a gastric wash.

A foreign-body obstruction commonly occurs in captive snakes that are housed on the improper substrate. Check your references, and use the proper substrates as mentioned in chapter 2. Towels, hand cloths, and T-shirts are not acceptable; they may be accidentally ingested. Incidentally, you can sometimes induce the vomiting of an ingested towel or hand cloth by lowering the cage temperature. Give the snake a sterile electrolyte solution intraperitoneally to counteract the dehydrating action of the towel. Then place the snake in a relatively cool area, about 50°F to 60°F (10°C to 16°C). Vomiting of these soft objects usually occurs within two to three days under these circumstances. You must monitor the snake for dehydration, and intraperitoneal fluids and antibiotics are advisable during and after this procedure. Note that this is a practical field approach to be used when sedation and endoscopic retrieval of the hand cloth are not possible. This approach is definitely worth considering before attempting surgical

This python is bloated from a foreign body impaction; it accidentally consumed a towel along with its meal. Never use towels for bedding in a snake cage.

retrieval, but you must carefully monitor the state of hydration in these animals. (In a seriously dehydrated snake, its skin has wrinkles that return very slowly or not at all to their original position when gently pulled away from the body.)

In older snakes, tumors are definitely a possible cause of regurgitation or vomiting. Your reptile-oriented veterinarian can determine if one is present by means of physical examination, endoscopic exam, X ray, or any combination of these.

Many snakes tend to drink heavily after gorging on a large meal. Sometimes, it appears that they may overdrink; vomiting or regurgitation occurs soon afterward.

Dehydration theoretically causes irritation to the lining of the gut by blocking the smooth passage of food because of the increased friction, thereby increasing the likelihood of vomiting or regurgitation.

When vomiting occurs, isolate the animal, restrict handling, lower the temperature of the enclosure as needed, feed less frequently and offer smaller prey, and make sure that the cage is clean and the food is fresh. If vomiting persists, have your snake examined by a reptile-oriented veterinarian, who may suggest a fecal exam, a culture and sensitivity test, or a biopsy to determine the cause or causes of the problem and the proper treatment.

CHAPTER 7

FEEDING PROBLEMS

R esearching your particular species' food preferences will be important in determining your feeding success with that species. Fortunately, most of the commonly maintained species will readily accept domestic mice as food, but some species may require food items that are difficult to procure. Such species are best left to the experts. You can train many species to accept a domestic rodent by rubbing a favored food item on it. This technique is called scent transferring or scenting and has been known to work extremely well (see the following section on dietary preference). However, it has yet to be determined whether domestic rodents represent a balanced long-term diet for snakes that normally eat other kinds of prey.

If a snake refuses rodents and must eat fish, the keeper must make every effort to provide whole, fresh fish or whole, fresh fish that have recently been frozen and thawed. Fish frozen for longer than three to six months have probably lost some of their nutrient value. Be aware

This snake is consuming a toad. Providing your snake with the right diet is essential for its health.

that diets made up solely of fish may predispose a captive snake to thiamine deficiency with resultant neurological symptoms. This deficiency may be avoided either by feeding a varied diet or by supplementing the fish diet with a supplement containing vitamin B_1, such as brewer's yeast. Dietary supplements are not normally necessary for snakes on a diet of whole rodents.

Weight Loss

Weight loss (or failure to gain) is another common complaint with captive snakes. As you might expect, parasites are high on the list of possible causes, but there are a number of other reasons this condition might occur; some are not immediately obvious, assuming that the animal is eating. Consider the following possible causes of weight loss.

Insufficient Amount of Food

If a snake is housed singly in the proper environment and has a good appetite yet loses weight, your first approach may be to try the obvious—offer more food. If this does not work, it is time to consider the other possibilities listed below.

If your snake isn't gaining weight, try offering it more food. If the problem persists, talk to your veterinarian.

Parasites

The variety of parasites is enormous, but basically they can be divided into two groups: (1) internal parasites, which include metazoans (worms) and protoza (one-celled organisms such as amoebas, flagellates, and coccidia); and (2) external parasites such as mites and ticks. Most of these parasites, whether they are internal or external, are either known to be or are strongly suspected of being quite harmful to their hosts and should be eliminated by your veterinarian. (This treatment to eliminate parasites is discussed in detail in chapter 5.) In herbivorous reptiles, some one-celled organisms are commensals or symbiotic (helpful to the host by aiding in the breakdown of food or in the production of vitamins), but this kind of parasitic interaction has not been determined in snakes (even though there is a possibility that intestinal bacteria contribute to the production of vitamin B_1). Certainly, the presence of these organisms in an animal that is losing weight and that has less-than-normal–appearing stools (loose or mucus laden) should make you suspicious. Frequent fecal exams are important.

Insectivorous snakes may not receive an adequate amount of digestible food. Consider offering soft-bodied insects, such as wax worms, recently molted mealworms and pupae, hairless caterpillars, and moths.

A Diet's Improper Caloric Content or Digestibility

Some foods are not very digestible. An insectivorous snake consuming a large percentage of beetles (and some of their larvae), mature crickets, and grasshoppers may be getting a larger percentage of indigestible material—namely, chitin—than it would if it were eating soft-bodied insects, younger insects, or recently molted or metamorphosed insects.

Maldigestion or Malabsorption

It is quite possible that a snake may not have the ability to digest or absorb its food. This problem may relate to a defect in the pancreas or gastrointestinal tract. The atrophy of the pancreas in vipers is one example of this kind of problem. Another is the hypertrophy (thickening of the lining) of parts of the gastrointestinal tract when infected by *Cryptosporidia*.

Increased Metabolic Rate Caused by High Environmental Temperature

A snake's metabolic rate rises with its body temperature; therefore, the caloric requirement for maintenance most likely will also increase when the body temperature elevates. A snake maintained in a room that is very warm will probably need nearly twice as much food as one maintained in a cooler room. Theoretically, there may be a high temperature range beyond which cool-climate snakes cannot eat sufficient quantities of food to maintain themselves when they are exposed to this heat for long periods of time. In fact, it has been suggested by some authorities that vitamin deficiencies may occur in some ectotherms maintained at high temperatures because different metabolic pathways occur at different rates; at constantly high temperatures, these ectotherms may use up vitamins in one reaction faster than they can be replaced.

You can avoid temperature-related problems by researching the preferred daily and seasonal temperatures of your particular species and keeping your snakes as near as possible to those temperatures. An example is the Andean milk snake (*Lampropeltis triangulum andesiana*), which lives in the wild at high elevations and requires lower ambient temperatures, 72°F to 75°F (22°C to 24°C). If such information on your species is not available, provide a temperature regime that is similar to the geographic area from which the animal originated. The use of thermal gradients within the enclosure is also important to allow the animal to thermoregulate (see also chapter 2).

Metabolic Rate Elevated by Endocrine Disorder
Endocrine disorders—such as primary hyperthyroidism, in which the thyroid gland is enlarged and secretes increased levels of thyroid hormone—may cause weight loss and dysecdysis (see chapter 3). If the diagnosis of hyperthyroidism is supported by an elevated T3 and T4 level, there are medications that may control this problem. We have successfully used methimazole at a dose of 1 milligram per kilogram of body weight per day for three weeks to break the rapid dysecdysis cycle. Interestingly, that snake did well for three months after the medication was stopped, even though it should have been continued on a daily basis. In mammals, the medication is administered every day for the life of the animal. This is a very rare disease in snakes, and to date we have observed it only in very old snakes. Before this diagnosis is made, the veterinarian will want to rule out other diseases, such as kidney disease or cancer, by running a complete blood screen and possibly x-raying.

Dehydration and Kidney Failure

Dehydration caused by a very dry environment and an improperly located water source can contribute to weight loss. Over time, kidney damage can result, which makes a snake unable to conserve body fluids and possibly lose protein through the urinary tract. For these reasons, you should provide water regularly to most snakes. (See also the discussion on excess humidity in chapter 2.) In addition, high-humidity refuges should be made available to most snakes. This is usually accomplished with a humidity box, a plastic box with a hole cut in the lid that has been stuffed with sphagnum moss lightly misted with water. The purpose of this box is to create a high-humidity retreat in an otherwise dry and well-ventilated environment. Failure to provide a high-humidity retreat may be a huge problem in snake herpetoculture. Unlike more obvious diseases, this chronic dehydration may take its toll slowly, resulting in the premature death of captive snakes. Though the cause of death may be listed as gout, or kidney disease, the actual cause of death was chronic dehydration of a cage that was clean, warm, and dry—just as the doctor ordered. Why is it that virtually all snakes with more permeable skin (garter snakes and water snakes among others) have an average captive longevity record of less than ten years, when those with less permeable skin (rattlesnakes) average twenty-five to thirty years? We know from natural history studies that even the tiny ringneck snake can live for twenty years in the wild, and the same is true for garter snakes. Their early demise in captivity is a warning to us that all snakes, especially young snakes of every species, should have a high-humidity retreat placed on the cool side of their cage.

Cancer Cachexia

Tumors can cause weight loss because the substances they sometimes produce may inhibit feeding and change the metabolism—the most severe cases resulting in cachexia, a physical wasting away and severe malnutrition. A regular checkup by your veterinarian may reveal suspicious masses, which in many cases can be successfully removed.

There are a number of reasons why a snake may be underweight, including environmental factors, stress, and illness.

Although these are some of the most likely reasons for weight loss, anorexia is by far the most common cause of weight loss in captive snakes. Next we will discuss several possible causes of anorexia in addition to other feeding problems.

Anorexia/Inappetence

Inappetence is the second most frustrating problem (after sudden death) that we deal with as herpetoculturists and veterinarians. There are a number of reasons for its occurrence and a number of solutions. We have grouped these reasons for purposes of our discussion, but several factors may be at play in any one case of anorexia.

Environmental Factors

Perhaps the most common reasons for failure to feed are related to the snake's environment. Fluctuation in temperature or humidity (which may be imperceptible to the owner), or both, may trigger a loss of appetite in a captive snake, even a long-term captive. Maintaining a snake in a cage with a thermal gradient that approaches its preferred optimum temperature range for day and night cycles helps regulate its appetite.

Shortening of the photophase (the light cycle) in the fall and winter also may be responsible for the sudden onset of inappetence. Even if artificial lighting is provided, inappetence may still occur if there is a window in the room where the snake is maintained; some species cue in on the natural light cycles, regardless of the amount of artificial light you offer. At the opposite extreme, excessive lighting (continuous light) can result in anorexia, too. The quality and intensity of the light you may provide may contribute to a loss of appetite if the light is not appropriate for a particular species or for an individual specimen. Seasonal barometric pressure variations have proven important in the activity patterns of some amphibians and reptiles, and presumably these variations may affect their appetite as well.

Remember that anorexia is a normal, self-protective mechanism for many temperate-zone reptiles in preparation for brumation (hibernation). Force-feeding during brumation is usually uncalled for and may result in trauma, leading to anorexia later. Temperate-zone snakes may stop eating for four to six months if exposed to lower temperatures, generally suffer no ill effects, and experience minimal weight loss.

The substrate is often found to be a cause in cases of anorexia. Certainly, secretive species—for example, Arizona coral snakes (*Micruroides euryxanthus*) and shovelnose snakes (*Chionactis* spp.)—may refuse to feed unless they are provided with a good burrowing medium such as mulch or sand. Similarly, arboreal snakes may refuse to feed if they are not provided with stable branches. Cage size is another extremely important captive environmental factor. Many a snake will begin feeding after it is placed in a larger or smaller cage, depending upon its needs. Of course, you should research all these factors before the arrival of the animal in question.

Dietary Preference Factors

Herpetoculturists have a general understanding of the basic dietary preferences of most species; however, individual snakes can have particular preferences that may not be readily available, and these preferences are discovered only by trial and error. However, there are many good references that one can refer to for the species in question. We strongly

Some snakes are very particular about their food. Despite your best efforts, you may not be able to transition them from lizards to rodents or from live to prekilled food.

encourage you to refer to a book summarizing the natural history of the species in question. Substitution of a snake's preferred food items may or may not be acceptable to the snake, and even mice and rats may not constitute a balanced diet for some species.

Examples of substitutes that are unacceptable to the palates of some captive snakes include wax worms instead of ants for some blind snakes (*Leptotyphlops* spp.) and domestic mice instead of lizards for some gray-banded kingsnakes (*Lampropeltis alterna*). Many herpetoculturists are ingenious at tricking their snakes into feeding by utilizing scent-transfer techniques by rubbing a preferred food item on a readily available domestic item. For example, some keepers rub a dead lizard or anole against the skin of a prekilled mouse before offering the rodent to a stubborn feeder. Another common trick is to stuff the tail of a prekilled feeder lizard into the mouth of a prekilled mouse, then offer the stuffed meal to the snake. Some specimens will take only dead food, whereas others will accept only live food and will starve to death if not provided with it. Some will take dead prey but only when you shake it in their faces by dangling the food with long tongs to simulate live prey. Some species, such as sharptail snakes (*Contia tenuis*) and rock rattlesnakes (*Crotalus lepidus*), are particular about the size of their prey.

Psychological Factors

Psychological factors have only recently received a great deal of attention from herpetoculturists. The particular placement of a cage, the enclosure's stability, and a snake's visibility of the goings-on outside the cage all may cause decreased appetite. The presence of more than one snake in the same cage may inhibit the feeding of a submissive one; of course, any snake's appetite may decrease if the species is naturally skittish or territorial. Frequent handling by the keeper, frequent passersby, and even frequent cleaning also may inhibit feeding. Prey sometimes may injure an otherwise good feeder, and as a result the snake becomes "mouse shy." Therefore, it is always advisable to house snakes singly, in stable cages, and with restricted visibility. Handle a snake less frequently if it is a finicky eater and, in most cases (except for insectivores), offer it prekilled prey whenever possible.

Periods of anorexia are natural for many snakes, particularly just prior to shedding and during the brumation period. Male snakes during breeding season and gestating female snakes also stop feeding as a matter of course.

Overfeeding a snake may cause fasting later on, but it is not a cause for concern. Some specimens binge and then fast as part of their normal eating habits, a process that may be tied to natural cycles of food availability in the wild.

Medical Factors

Medical reasons for anorexia in reptiles are numerous. Perhaps the most common reason is parasites, especially in wild-caught reptiles. Long-term captives also are vulnerable if they either have never been treated or have not been treated recently. We strongly advise regular fecal exams and treatments as needed. However, if fecals are not available at the time of an exam or cannot be obtained by a cloacal wash, then we often administer a routine deworming with fenbendazole annually. The dose is listed in the tables in chapter 16.

Intestinal impactions caused by the ingestion of improper substrates, such as small-size gravel or ground corncob, are a close second cause of anorexia in smaller snakes.

Infections involving any or all systems—including respiratory, intestinal, or integumentary—are other common reasons for inappetence. We can certainly understand how a snake with a bad case of stomatitis or pneumonia may not have the desire to feed, but any infection also is capable of causing anorexia. Metabolic problems caused by excesses or deficiencies of various minerals, vitamins, or hormones also may cause appetite loss; one example is hyperthyroidism in older rat snakes (genus *Elaphe*). Health problems such as diabetes, kidney failure, tumors, trauma, and toxins can all cause anorexia as well.

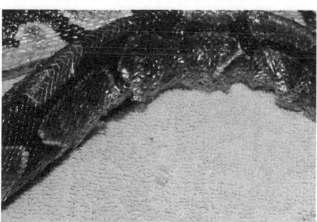

This snake is starving to death. As a snake's health declines, it lacks sufficient protein to complete its shed.

Sensory loss (especially loss of the extremely important senses of smell and sight) may account for an inexplicable failure to feed. Check for an intact tongue in a recently captured snake that shows interest only in live, moving prey and never in prekilled prey. Incidentally, sight does not seem as important as smell in the feeding response of many snakes. Yet the feeding patterns of large-eyed diurnal snakes, which are very visually oriented, may be expected to be negatively affected by the loss of one or both eyes, through trauma or infection.

One pleasant medical reason for anorexia in female snakes is that they are gravid. As the embryos develop, they occupy a good deal of space in the animal's body, and some believe this condition inhibits feeding. Pregnancy is not so pleasant, however, if an anorexic gravid female is very malnourished, has a severe infection that has spread to the uterus, or has some other life-threatening difficulty that may lead to dystocia (egg-binding), yolk emboli, yolk peritonitis, uterine rupture, retained products of conception, infertility, or death.

Dehydration

The most common causes of dehydration are lack of drinking water and consistently high temperatures inside the cage. Some materials used to construct cages and some types of substrates will also contribute to dehydration.

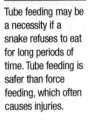

Tube feeding may be a necessity if a snake refuses to eat for long periods of time. Tube feeding is safer than force feeding, which often causes injuries.

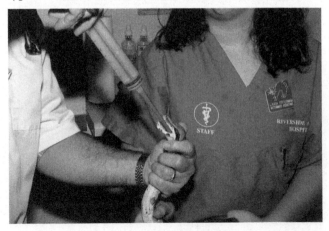

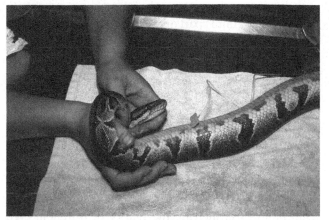

A veterinarian rehydrates a severely dehydrated snake by using an intracardiac catheter.

Bare, untreated wood cages are notoriously hygroscopic (absorbent of air humidity) as well as abrasive and difficult to disinfect. Substrates such as corncob litter are also hygroscopic. Therefore, we advise the keeper to avoid wooden cages, drying substrates, and excessive heat. House your snakes in smooth-sided enclosures constructed of nonporous materials such as glass, plastic, metal, or melamine-coated wood. Consult up-to-date resources for tips from other herpetoculturists on the specific water provisions and substrate preferences that work best for the species you keep.

If a snake, particularly a small one, appears seriously dehydrated (its skin has wrinkles that return very slowly or not at all to their original position when gently pulled away from the body), you should get the snake to a veterinarian right away. It may need emergency fluids or tube feeding. If you cannot reach a veterinarian immediately, you may administer an electrolyte solution such as dilute Pedialyte (mix it with an equal quantity of water to produce a half-strength solution) through a stomach tube (about 2 to 3 milliliters per 100 grams of body weight per day for several days, or until seen by a veterinarian). A veterinarian will administer about 20 milliliters of a sterile electrolyte solution per kilogram of body weight intraperitoneally (or subcutaneously if the snake is large enough), once per day for several days. Note: an injection in the abdominal cavity must be done with caution; administer injections only in the caudal (last third) part of the body to avoid puncturing abdominal structures and lungs. The most frequent solution used is lactated Ringer's, although Jarchow's (1998) recommendation, 2 parts 2.5 percent dextrose in 0.45 percent salt plus 1 part Ringer's, is theoretically a better alternative. We prefer to use the readily available 2.5 percent dextrose in 0.45 percent sodium chloride as the standard for most dehydrated reptiles. Extremely dehydrated snakes may benefit from an intracardiac catheter as perfected by Mader (pers. comm.).

Keep the snake warm, but remember that increased temperatures will increase the rate of dehydration, even though it will improve the snake's ability to use the fluids administered. Remember, it is sometimes difficult to differentiate between a very thin snake (that is, one suffering from starvation) and a dehydrated snake.

Feeding Frequency

One of the questions most commonly asked of reptile veterinarians is how frequently a snake should be fed. This is an important question and its answer has been arrived at in several ways.

Calculating Maintenance Levels

Studies of wild snakes have revealed that temperate-zone snakes generally consume two to four times their body weight in food per year (Fitch 1982). Inactive species and individuals were expected to have requirements closer to the bottom end of this range, whereas very active snakes were expected to have requirements closer to the upper end. Using this information as a guideline and considering that most captive snakes get little exercise in captivity, the average 1-pound (0.45 kg) snake would require 2 pounds (1 kg) of mice per year. It would take approximately eighteen mice (at an average weight of 50 grams each) per year to maintain a 1-pound snake. Assuming an eight-month period of activity and feeding and four months of brumation, this formula translates to one mouse every two weeks to maintain a

Occasionally, a snake becomes so malnourished that its skin wrinkles and splits.

1-pound snake. Remember that this calculated amount is for a sluggish or inactive snake and does not supply the extra energy that reproduction or growth may require.

Using another approach, one can calculate the energy requirement of a snake based upon its metabolic rate. The energy required in kilocalories (kcal) equals ten times the animal's body weight in kilograms to the 0.75 power. Hence, a 1-pound (0.45 kg) snake would require 5.5 kcal per day. Because a mouse contains about 85 kcal, one mouse would meet the energy requirements of a 1-pound snake for approximately two weeks (Mader 1993), excluding energy for growth or reproduction.

These two methods are reasonably close to predicting the maintenance needs of a 1-pound snake. However, these levels are far exceeded by most snake keepers, especially snake breeders who, understandably, are trying to supply a great deal of excess energy for growth and reproduction. Commonly, obesity is the result, especially after the snake's reproduction stops and the intense feeding regime continues. Males seem to be much more prone to obesity than egg-laying females, thereby supporting the contention of many herpetoculturists that the energy requirements of females may be much higher than those of males. This belief is also supported by our observations, and by those of many others, that females of many species are less difficult to please than males of the same species. Perhaps females' greater energy demands require that they feed more consistently and with less obvious prey preference than males. (Sexual differences of snakes are discussed in detail in Seigel and Collins 1993.)

Obesity caused by overfeeding and inactivity is a common problem in captive snakes. Don't, however, put your snake on a crash diet. Talk to a reptile veterinarian about a safe feeding regimen.

Managing Obesity

How can you tell if a snake is obese? The two most common signs of obesity are (1) exposed skin between the scales, and (2) inability to coil properly. Another sign of obesity that we have observed is the presence of "fat lines." These are vertical folds in the scales created when a very heavy snake remains coiled for long periods of time. The excess fat creates folds much like "love handles" in humans, and the scales in the folds bend backward and become creased.

Obesity in snakes has been associated with a number of serious health risks. These include heart disease, tumors, low fertility, metabolic problems, and musculoskeletal problems. Longevity in captivity is also likely to be reduced in obese animals. Therefore, we strongly advise you to feed your snake no more than is necessary for the function needed. Maintenance levels can be calculated using the formula previously cited, but diets for reproduction or growth may require two to three times that amount. Feeding much more than this will usually cause your snake to become seriously overweight.

If a snake is diagnosed as obese, you may place it on a weight-loss diet. Gradually reduce the snake's food intake down to maintenance levels. To do so, you will need to calculate the maintenance amount as previously discussed, basing your calculation on the optimum weight of the snake, and then reducing slowly toward that amount over several months: For example, if a snake is obese and the maintenance amount is calculated at one mouse per week yet the snake is presently receiving three mice per week, reduce the amount fed as follows: For the first month, reduce the amount fed by 25 percent (12 mice per month × 0.75 = 8 mice per month). The next month, reduce the amount fed by another 25 percent (8 × 0.75 = 6 mice per month). By the third month, you can usually approach the maintenance level safely. Weigh the snake as frequently as possible to monitor progress.

Never put an obese snake on a starvation diet as it could cause a number of gastrointestinal or metabolic problems, even though these are rare.

CHAPTER 8

REPRODUCTION

P articularly frustrating in the life of a herpetoculturist is the persistent failure of the snakes in his or her care to reproduce. There are many reasons this failure occurs; fortunately, there are also many solutions. The reasons for failure to reproduce are numerous and complex, but here we will simplify them by dividing them into three categories. These are premating problems, mating problems, and postmating problems.

Premating Problems

Premating problems involve environmental factors such as cage size, lighting, temperature gradient, humidity, diet, and the duration of and temperature range during brumation (hibernation). The age and overall health of your snake are also important in determining whether it will mate and whether it can produce viable offspring. Animals that are not well adapted to captivity or are in poor condition for reasons such as parasitism or previous overbreeding are not likely to produce viable eggs or sperm.

Reproductive problems have many causes, including poor husbandry, improper temperature, and faulty sexing.

Brumation, or hibernation, is very important for the reproductive health of many temperate-zone snakes. Length of brumation, temperature during brumation, and dehydration during brumation can all affect a snake's ability to reproduce.

Improper temperatures (at either extreme) for too long, or the proper temperature for too short a time, are well-known causes of infertility in snakes of both sexes. To provide the proper temperature, humidity, diet, and so forth, you must research the specific needs of the species that you keep; in some cases, you will learn through trial and error. As a general rule, the minimum duration of brumation for most temperate-zone snakes is ten weeks at a temperature range of 40°F to 55°F (4°C to 13°C). Tropical snakes are never brumated. They are exposed to several months of lower nighttime temperatures (usually no lower than 72°F, 22°C), and the photoperiod is decreased (usually to about ten hours) to cycle them to breed. Again, this is a general guideline. Research your species!

Mating Problems

The mating process itself usually depends upon the environmental and husbandry factors discussed above and upon the environmental cues present at the time of the mating. Temperature, humidity, barometric pressure, cage complexity, and time of day may be critical in determining whether mating will occur. To mate, recently captured animals may require much more complex environmental cues than long-term captives require (Ross and Marzec 1990).

Another factor is the social or behavioral environment. Since every animal is an individual, any snake may be

99

incompatible with another. Some species require the presence of multiple males or females in order to mate consistently in captivity. Specific olfactory, visual, and tactile cues certainly play a major part in successful mating behavior, even though olfactory and tactile cues seem to be far more important than visual cues in many of the snakes studied to date (Gillingham 1987).

Missexing is a very common reason for the failure of two snakes to mate. Double-check the sex of both snakes prior to breeding season. If you are not sure, have them sexed by an experienced herpetoculturist or veterinarian.

Finally, previous trauma to or infection of the caudal spine or reproductive system (often unknown to the owner) may severely hinder any reproductive effort. One good example is a fracture of the spine near the cloacal region of a snake, which prevents the proper alignment of its cloaca with its partner during attempted copulation. Such individuals may attempt mating for days without success.

Once mating has occurred, fertilization of the ova is possible, but it is not definite. Consequently, timing is critical

The Thermal Gradient

There should be a thermal gradient available in every cage because males and females may choose different temperatures at certain times for different functions.

for many temperate-zone or so-called seasonal snakes, and you should make every effort to "synchronize" the pairs in your care by cycling them through the same temperature and photoperiod regime (Seigel, Collins, and Novak 1987).

Postmating Problems

Assuming that viable eggs and sperm were produced and that copulation occurred at the appropriate time, there are still a number of things that can, and frequently do, go wrong. Poor nutritional status, invasion by parasites, stress, frequent handling, inappropriate temperature gradient, or infection can cause a female to be infertile or have reduced litter sizes. Radiation (from X rays), toxins (including some antibiotics), and trauma can also affect fertility in both sexes. In smaller species of live-bearing snakes, stress, especially caused by handling, may cause spontaneous abortions.

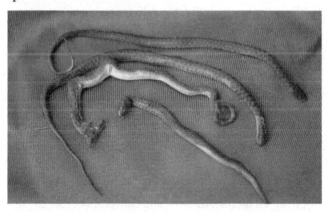

Improper temperatures, an unhealthy mother, or environmental toxins can lead to birth defects.

Within a species, clutch size and weight of the young are directly correlated with the weight of the female, even though the weight of the young and clutch size are often inversely related to each other; in other words, the greater the number of eggs or young produced, the smaller the size of each (Seigel, Collins, and Novak 1987). Thus, there is a theoretical body mass below which a female will produce only very sickly young, if she's able to produce at all. Breeding a female with poor body mass may seriously compromise her life.

This red rat snake is egg-bound. Your snake may be egg-bound if she hasn't delivered her eggs two weeks after her prelaying shed, she begins laying eggs and then stops before delivering all the eggs, or she has an egg in her vent for more than three hours.

Dystocia (Egg-Binding)

The retained products of a previous reproductive effort in certain female snakes can prevent the normal development of otherwise healthy embryos. Dystocia (also called egg-binding) is an inability to deliver eggs or live young once the eggs are formed. Dystocia is a common malady of oviparous (eggs develop and hatch outside the maternal body) and ovoviviparous (eggs develop within the maternal body) snakes.

Dystocia is frequently related to an improper environment caused by inadequate temperatures, lack of privacy, improper laying medium, and so on. Other causes include handling of the snake, the snake's age and size, muscle tone, obesity, large egg size, infections, improper nutrition, parasites, structural defects (torsion of uterus, ruptured uterus, or prolapsed uterus), tumors, and dehydration. (See the following section on egg care for more detailed information on how to prepare a snake and her environment for successful egg deposition.) If dystocia occurs, you should regard it as a medical emergency that must be treated within a few days—the sooner the better!

A snake may be egg-bound if any of the following conditions apply:

1. If she has failed to deliver her eggs by the end of the normal gestation period for her species. Because this period varies greatly as a result of a number of

environmental factors, many herpetoculturists assume that a snake is egg-bound if she has not laid her eggs within two weeks after the prelaying shed, rather than after a set gestation period.

2. If she started laying and then stopped abruptly while still containing eggs.

3. If she is straining, appears irritable or agitated, and has one or more eggs stuck at her vent for more than three hours. Under these circumstances, consider the following measures: (a) if no ventral heat is provided, add some with a gentle ventral heat source such as a heating pad or a heat strip, (b) make sure that the snake has a suitable private place in which to lay eggs such as an egg-laying box, (c) provide drinking water, and (d) consider temporarily raising the humidity in your snake's enclosure. If these measures fail, warm water soaks or enemas are the next steps and the least invasive treatment techniques.

The following procedures should be performed only by an experienced reptile veterinarian. One of the first steps that many veterinarians take is to administer an injection of calcium. Brown and Martin (1990) recommend a flat dose of 50 milligrams of calcium gluconate intramuscularly, which may be repeated several times over the course of twenty-four hours. Lloyd (1992) suggests a dose of 2 to 5 milligrams per kilogram of body weight intramuscularly or

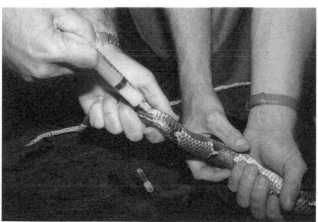

A veterinarian aspirates the egg to allow the snake to deliver the empty shell in a process called ovocentesis.

subcutaneously of Calphosan (10 mg per mL). We routinely use Calphosan (calcium glycerophosphate) for this purpose. The rationale is that malnourished snakes may have a calcium deficiency and therefore have poor muscle tone. Finally, if these measures do not result in the passage of eggs, you should consider chemical induction.

Induction of the egg-laying process in snakes has taken a major step forward with the use of vasotocin rather than oxytocin. Certainly, oxytocin at a dose of two units per 100 grams has been effective in some cases, but there also have been many cases in which it was not. Since vasotocin is so much more effective, it has rapidly become the agent of choice for induction of egg laying in egg-bound snakes. Lloyd (1992) suggests a dose of 0.01 to 1 milligram per kilogram of body weight intraperitoneally. The problem is that vasotocin is an experimental drug that is not widely available at this time. If this procedure is unsuccessful, a prudent next step is ovocentesis of the caudalmost egg (inserting a needle into the egg nearest the cloaca and aspirating its contents) and repeating the dose of vasotocin or oxytocin. Note: The ovocentesis procedure is not without risk to the mother. As Mader (1989) points out, the procedure not only will cause the death of the embryo if it is viable (bound eggs are almost never viable) but also can result in peritonitis (an infection in the abdominal cavity of the mother) if it allows material from the egg to leak into the abdominal cavity. Mader also warns against this procedure being carried out in a nonsterile manner; the actual insertion of the needle may result in a lethal bacterial infection. Therefore, this procedure should be avoided unless it is absolutely necessary, and sterile techniques must be used if it is attempted. Scrub the area to be perforated with a povidone-iodine scrub, then wipe with alcohol several times before inserting a sterile needle. A 22-gauge needle on a 6- or 12-cc syringe is usually sufficient for this purpose in a kingsnake or corn snake, but an 18-gauge needle on a 60-cc syringe may be required for a python. It is important to note that the use of oxytocin or vasotocin can be fatal if the cause of dystocia is an

Cleft scutes, as seen in this ball python, are a congenital defect that usually means there was a problem during incubation.

adhesion or a torsion of the uterus. The female overstrains and the uterus may tear. Many veterinarians advise against its use until all other methods have been tried.

Once the caudalmost egg is perforated and its contents removed, a gentle manual expression may deliver it from the uterus. If not, do not force the egg; forcing may cause severe, irreversible damage and the female's inability to reproduce in the future or even result in her death. Klingenberg (1991) advises against manipulation of the drained egg, suggesting that the snake should be placed back in its cage and left alone while the calcium and oxytocin (or vasotocin) are allowed to work. We believe this is appropriate if the egg is up high. However, if the egg is near the cloaca, then gentle and careful manipulation of the egg is acceptable. Manipulating a perforated egg may increase the risk of leakage of its contents, but then again, so will inefficient uterine contractions. If the perforated egg is delivered, place the snake back into the appropriate environment, and let the calcium and vasotocin work on the rest of the eggs before attempting any more manipulation. If the female fails to lay any eggs within twelve hours of this procedure, surgery is advisable. If she lays some eggs, you may wish to repeat the previous treatment until all eggs are out. Antibiotics also are always advisable after ovocentesis and before surgery.

105

Good medical and surgical intervention may save a snake, but the best medicine, as we have emphasized throughout this book, is prevention through proper husbandry.

Late-Stage Developmental Problems

If the young survive the initial stage of development, there is still a risk of death or deformity during the later stages. In oviparous species, the risk of death and deformity during incubation is significant. Desiccation, overhydration, lack of oxygen, exposure to temperature extremes, fungal infection, and predation by fly larvae are all common causes for the destruction of embryos within the egg. The proper incubation techniques and temperatures are discussed later in this chapter. You may need to research further for specific information on your snake's species.

Common Mistakes by the Herpetoculturist

Once you have worked out all of the intricacies of male and female husbandry, you should avoid some of the all-too-common traps of modern herpetoculture. These include pushing animals to breed when they are very young, inducing females to produce more than one clutch in a breeding season, and inbreeding generation after generation. Inbreeding may be especially devastating to young females, the most frequent victims of dystocia. Klingenberg (1991) refers to these young obese animals as "lumps" and suggests that their poor muscle tone, a result of inactivity, overfeeding, and overbreeding, is a major cause of their dystocia.

The herpetoculturist must remember that reproduction is a luxury for a captive snake. Only if all of the animal's other needs are met will it reproduce successfully. Only if there is excess energy available to your snake will some of it be channeled into a successful and healthy reproductive effort, yet some emaciated snakes will breed much to their detriment. You must first make every effort to successfully maintain the snake in question, then work on breeding. We are dismayed when we see the poor condition of so-called breeder snakes presented to us by inexperienced herpetoculturists. Breeder snakes should be in peak physical condition, of the proper age and size, and kept in the appropriate environment. If these conditions are met, successful reproduction is almost inevitable. Problems arise and failures occur only rarely under such circumstances. The biggest problem, then, is trying to determine just what the appropriate environment is. We cannot overemphasize that environmental factors play a crucial role in all categories of mating problems and in almost every facet of maintenance as well.

Breeding and Egg Care

Although we do not intend this book to be a breeding manual, the deposition of eggs may thrust the snake keeper into a critical situation that requires immediate attention. We provide the following information to assist in the proper delivery of eggs and their care, once they are discovered. This is a cursory discussion of egg care and not intended as a review of all incubation techniques and problems. Refer to any of the excellent references and magazine articles available for more specific information on the care of the eggs of a particular snake species.

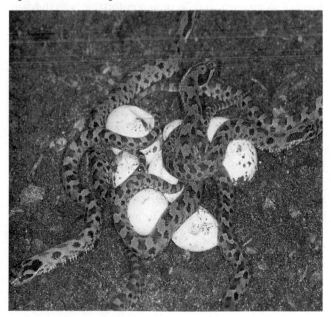

Provide your snake a nesting box with a semimoist nesting material, such as sphagnum moss or vermiculite.

Nesting Site

Most female snakes will require a suitable nesting site. Otherwise, they will refuse to lay their eggs or will lay them in inappropriate places, such as in their water bowls, which will lead to the embryos' drowning from excess water absorption. For most snakes, a nesting site will consist of a secluded area with a semimoist medium. Sphagnum moss and vermiculite, lightly mixed with water, have both been used as egg-laying media with excellent success. For most snakes, plastic shoeboxes or sweater boxes make ideal egg-laying boxes. Simply cut a small hole in the lid or one side of the box. (Top holes are preferable because many snakes, in an effort to find the best spot in which to lay their eggs, will push much of the medium out of a hole punched in the side of the box.) Secure the top well or the snake may pop it off. Some people have used large plastic dog carriers or cat carriers for larger snakes such as pythons. Plastic sheets may be taped over the holes in these carriers to reduce humidity loss.

Place the egg-laying box in the cage several days to a few weeks prior to expected egg laying, to allow the female to learn of its presence and become comfortable with it. Many snakes have what has been termed a prelaying shed within two to four weeks of egg laying.

Incubation

Once the eggs are deposited, move them to an incubation box. (Some python keepers choose to leave the eggs with the mother for incubation, but this is risky unless the temperature and humidity of the cage are reasonably close to proper levels. However, if you can keep the ambient temperature above 80°F [27°C] and the humidity above 90 percent, the female python will often do the rest, raising the temperature of the clutch to around 90°F with her muscle contractions.) Incubation boxes are commonly airtight containers in which the snake keeper has placed a vermiculite and water mixture. The ratio of the mixture has been the topic of a great deal of discussion recently, but we find that a ratio of less than one part water to one part vermiculite (by weight)

Once your snake has laid her eggs, move the eggs to an incubator where you can control temperature and humidity. Eggs that begin to cave in, like the ones shown here, may be suffering from an incubator that is too dry.

is suitable. Some authorities have suggested that a ratio of one-half part water to one part vermiculite (by weight) is more likely to result in bigger, healthier babies (Hammack 1991). Many other substrates have been used, and these are discussed in detail in many other references.

The incubation period generally ranges from thirty to ninety days for most snakes, depending upon the species. Suitable incubation temperatures for pythons range from 88°F to 91°F (31°C to 33°C), whereas suitable incubation temperatures for most colubrids fluctuate from 70°F to 88°F (21°C to 31°C). You must remember to open the incubator frequently (five minutes every two to three days) during incubation to allow some air to enter the incubation box. Oxygen requirements are believed to increase as the embryos develop; therefore, you should probably increase the frequency of opening toward the latter part of the incubation period. Indeed, some herpetoculturists have proposed that failure to do so is likely responsible for late-term death of an embryo in the egg. Be certain not to cause excess vibration or rotation of the eggs. Snake eggs are never to be rotated; rotating them may kill the embryos.

If the eggs begin to cave in during the first few weeks of incubation, the incubating medium may be too dry, so make sure that they are set up as we have described. You may wish to add a small amount of water to the vermiculite surrounding the eggs to see if they "puff up." Another common reason eggs cave in is that they are infertile. If "weeping" (seeping of liquid from the surface) of the eggs occurs in early incubation, it usually means the eggs were laid prematurely and are most likely to die. Generally speaking, if the egg retains its shape, the young snake is probably still alive. We usually recommend giving all eggs the benefit of the doubt and not disturbing them until after the other eggs in the clutch have started to hatch.

Late-term death of fully developed embryos is a frustrating and common occurrence in snake egg incubation at the time of this writing. Presently, it is believed that this may be caused by an oxygen deficiency as previously discussed.

The Hatch

Normal hatching usually takes several days as the snakes pip (slice through their eggs) and remain in the egg while they convert from egg-membrane respiration to pulmonary respiration. Thus, you must not remove the young snakes from these eggs prematurely. If most of the eggs have hatched and one or two healthy-appearing ones remain unpipped, you may decide to intervene. Carefully slice the top of the egg to create a small window, and peer into the egg. You can do this with a pair of surgical forceps and a scalpel. Grasp the top of the shell with forceps and gently pull upward. Then gently incise the "tented" area (the area you have raised with the forceps) with the scalpel. Carefully extend the incision, the length of which will depend on the size of the egg, but usually about 1/2 to 2/3 of the length of the egg is adequate. Then extend it at a right angle from the initial incision. It has been our experience that the embryo is likely to be alive if clear albumen is rapidly expelled from the egg. Thickened or milky albumen that is not rapidly expelled is usually

---

Carrion Fly Infestation of Unhatched Eggs

Carrion flies may lay eggs inside snake eggs that have pipped but have not yet hatched, thereby threatening the young snakes. For this reason, we usually keep the top on our egg-laying boxes right through hatching, even though we remove and replace it frequently in the process of checking on the hatchlings.

This baby snake begins emerging from its shell. It generally takes a few days for snakes to hatch.

indicative of a dead embryo. If you observe a live snake, leave it alone and allow it several more days to emerge from the egg; some individuals take longer than others. When the snake does emerge, check it for an egg tooth. Some herpeto-culturists have suggested that many of these nonhatching live snakes are lacking an egg tooth. If this is true, and it turns out to be a genetic deficiency, saving the snake and breeding it may introduce a tremendously harmful gene into the captive snake population. As yet, however, the cause of this defect is undetermined for certain.

House hatchling snakes in a manner similar to that of adults, keeping in mind that access to a high-humidity area is especially important for hatchlings. A simple plastic container stuffed with semimoist sphagnum moss works well. These are called humidity boxes, but actually they are the same as the egg-laying boxes previously described. Hatchlings will usually shed within a few weeks, some as early as a few days. They may refuse food until after their first shed. (See also chapter 12.)

CHAPTER 9

RESPIRATORY PROBLEMS

E arly signs of respiratory problems, such as sneezing or a mild hissing noise, may signify an infection, although this is not necessarily the case. A chemical irritant such as that found in cedar shavings and cigarette smoke, high ammonia levels in dirty cages, or an allergen, such as the dust on corncob litter, may produce mild sinusitis, with consequent respiratory signs. So there may be no infection to treat, only an environment to correct. Swelling of the head region and skin around the nares just prior to shedding may be accompanied by wheezing, and an agitated snake may produce sharp, short hissing noises. Because both of these observations may be mistaken for signs of a respiratory infection, you should observe your snake carefully after a shed, while it is at rest.

This snake exhibits three of the four major signs of respiratory illness in snakes: an elevated head, a swollen throat, and open-mouth breathing. The other sign is increased mucous discharge from the mouth.

Diagnosing and Treating Respiratory Infections

More serious and characteristic signs of a respiratory infection (although not specifically present only in respiratory infections) in a snake are open-mouth breathing, a puffed-out throat, a raised head, and increased mucus in the mouth resulting in bubble blowing. Should a bona fide bacterial infection exist, bacteria may be secondary to another invader—such as a fungus, a parasite, or a virus. A respiratory infection may also occur in a snake with an already compromised immune system. The bacteria cultured from the trachea or oropharynx of these ill snakes are usually of the same gram negative group as that cultured from the skin. Therefore, the same approach is called for—environmental correction and supplemental heat are always the first steps in treating a suspected respiratory infection in snakes. If you see little improvement, don't wait too long before getting a snake to a reptile-oriented veterinarian for initiation of antibiotic therapy.

Besides antibiotics, there have been several discoveries over the past few years that have improved a snake's chances of surviving a serious case of pneumonia. T. H. Boyer (1992) found that atropine at a dose of 0.02 to 0.04 milligrams per kilogram of body weight injected subcutaneously twice per day was much more successful when treating "moist pneumonias." (Presumably, Dr. Boyer was referring to respiratory infections that had more mucus than others he had observed.) Qualls (1989) observed that Alupent (metaproterenol sulfate), which is a bronchodilator, eases respirations when a concentration of 0.6 percent Alupent is nebulized (administered as a fine mist) for ten minutes per treatment three times per day. Qualls also observed that one drop nebulized in a small amount of water would help to dry up mucus as well. Dr. Klingenberg warns that atropine should be used only if absolutely necessary; he has seen gut atony (poor muscle tone and bloating) in some snakes in which this was used (pers. comm.).

Viral Infections

Several viruses have been associated with respiratory disease in snakes. Perhaps the most notorious viral infection of snakes is paramyxovirus, which has affected large numbers of viperid and elapid snakes in collections around the country. This virus usually causes acute pneumonia as well as signs of neurological problems and results in death within several days. Another virus that causes severe and chronic respiratory signs is viral encephalitis of boid snakes, or the VEBS virus. In boas, VEBS causes signs of respiratory infection. In pythons, it causes progressive signs of neurological problems, such as incoordination and weakness. VEBS is also known as inclusion body disease (IBD). The outcome of either infection is usually death. We suspect that there may be numerous other viral diseases in snakes that may not be quite as severe and from which most snakes recover; however, we do not know for certain. A viral infection may respond partially to increased environmental heat, which will stimulate the snake's immune system, but deadly viruses such as paramyxovirus will require prompt and aggressive veterinary care if the snake is to have a fighting chance.

Pneumonia

Fungal pneumonias occur more frequently than most herpetoculturists or reptile veterinarians would like to believe. They are commonly misdiagnosed as nonresponsive

This snake is gasping for breath; it may be suffering from pneumonia.

Nasal and oral discharge, such as that seen on this snake, is another sign of respiratory illness.

bacterial pneumonias, but they are treatable, although treatment is sometimes difficult or expensive. Desert snakes housed in plastic containers with poor ventilation seem especially prone to fungal pneumonias, but any snake housed in moist conditions for long is a prime candidate. One western hooknose snake (*Gyalopion canum*), having been housed in a plastic shoebox for two months, died with signs of respiratory problems. However, a necropsy revealed fungal hyphae in the lung tissue. We have seen a number of wild snakes that have suspicious-looking lesions when they have been captured in low, wet areas or after weeks of very rainy weather. We have successfully applied amphotericin B in a nebulizer at the dose recommended by Jacobson (1988), which is 5 milligrams in 150 milliliters of saline solution nebulized for one hour twice per day for one week. Fluconazole, at a dose of 10 milligrams per kilogram of body weight orally once daily for two to three weeks has also proven effective for treating fungal infections in snakes.

Lung Parasites

Although not as common as gastrointestinal parasites, lung parasites are commonly present and may be a source of significant damage to your snake's lungs. Perhaps the most common lung invaders are the nematodes of the genus *Rhabdias*. Fortunately, as part of their life cycle, their eggs and larvae are frequently shed in the snake's stool, even

115

though the primary infection of *Rhabdias* is in the lung, thereby making a diagnosis easier. Unfortunately, neither the larvae of the genus *Rhabdias* nor that of *Strongyloides* can be readily distinguished in a stool smear. Your veterinarian can make a presumptive diagnosis by performing a tracheal wash or by reviewing the primary problem of the snake. A positive tracheal wash or a history of primarily respiratory signs would suggest *Rhabdias*, whereas a negative tracheal wash with a history of primarily gastrointestinal signs would suggest *Strongyloides*. The presence of any rhabditiform larvae (a term for the larvae of both genera) in the stool should be noted as such, and treatment should be initiated. No group of worms appears more widespread among captive snakes than the rhabditiform larvae. We have found this type of worm in more than twenty species of snakes, including South American cribos (genus *Drymarchon*), African ball pythons (*Python regius*), Asian reticulated pythons (*Python reticulates*), black-striped snakes (*Coniophanes imperialis*) from southern Texas, rosy boas (*Lichanura trivirgata trivirgata*) from Arizona, and kingsnakes (genus *Lampropeltis*) from Florida. Hence, you should examine all snakes carefully and use the appropriate dewormer. Among these are ivermectin and fenbendazole, at doses listed in the drug chart in chapter 16.

Pentastomids

Pentastomids are another type of parasite that may occur in the lungs or under the skin. Diagnosis of these parasites is a very serious matter for two reasons: first, they are capable of infecting people; second, there is presently no known treatment for these worms, either in snakes or in people, except surgical removal. It is for this reason that many veterinarians suggest euthanasia for these snakes, once they spot the characteristic five-hooked embryonated eggs during a fecal exam. Junge and Miller (1992) discuss respiratory diseases in reptiles and their treatment in more detail.

CHAPTER 10

NEUROLOGICAL PROBLEMS

Signs of neurological problems that we commonly observe in snakes include seizures, tremors, incoordination, weakness, "star gazing," blindness, and flaccid paralysis. In snakes, these signs usually are related to one of three things: infection, toxins, or a metabolic defect or deficiency. Trauma to the head or spine and overheating may also result in neurological symptoms.

A severe infection that involves brain tissues or that produces toxins affecting the brain is the most likely reason for obvious neurological symptoms such as seizures, tremors, or incoordination. Star gazing, where a snake arcs its head upward as if it is looking at the stars, is considered to be a sign specific to encephalitis (inflammation of the brain). Amoebic encephalitis (infection of the brain by an amoeba) is one of the causes of this sign. You should be especially suspicious of an infection (as opposed to trauma

This snake is star gazing (arching Its head upward as though looking up at the stars), a sign that usually indicates encephalitis.

Other symptoms of neurological problems are protruding eyes, weakness, and seizures.

or chemical toxicity) as the cause of neurological signs if the infection is accompanied by other signs, such as pneumonia or stomatitis. Bacterial infections may respond to treatment, but viral and amoebic infections are difficult to treat. The VEBS (now more commonly known as IBD) virus causes such symptoms, and there is no effective treatment. Toxins such as those found in insecticides (including pest strips with Vapona, if used improperly), paint, some medicines, and bacterial toxins may all cause signs of neurological disorder.

Treatment of bacterial infections of the brain can be successful with some of the antibiotics listed in the antibiotic charts in chapter 16. Amoebic infections of the brain may respond to metronidazole treatment. Refer to the charts for the doses. Viral infections may respond to supportive care (fluids), antibiotics for secondary infections, force-feeding if required, a good source of heat, and time. Keep in mind that an infection outside the brain or nervous system can cause signs that mimic an infection inside the brain or nervous system. This occurs because toxins produced by bacteria can act upon the brain. Thus, antibiotic treatment is always indicated and often successful. Don't give up.

Lastly, fish-eating snakes are prone to thiamin (vitamin B_1) deficiency. In snakes on a diet of fish alone, the deficiency may cause seizures within six months, if the diet is not supplemented with a vitamin and mineral powder. A thiamin deficiency may be prevented by feeding your snake a varied diet, including fish-scented, prekilled mice if possible, or by placing a small piece of a Brewer's yeast tablet inside some of the prekilled fish that you feed to your snake. Should your snake exhibit a tremendous increase in nervous behavior followed by seizures, administer between 0.05 and 0.1 cc of Tech America's Multi B Complex intramuscularly. This drug usually halts the symptoms within a matter of hours. The treatment and prognosis for recovery vary considerably with nerve problems. Bacterial infections may respond nicely to the appropriate antibiotics, while fewer snakes will survive an amoebic or viral encephalitis.

To treat toxicity, you must remove the toxin as well as the snake from its immediate environment. Washing the snake with soap and water may help. Atropine, at Boyer's (1992) recommended dose of 0.02 to 0.04 milligrams per kilogram, may be helpful in cases of organophosphate toxicity. After this treatment, give the snake fluids and supplemental heat. Note that metronidazole and ivermectin both are capable of causing neurological symptoms if given at much higher than recommended doses.

Use mite-control products with caution; make sure that snake cages are well ventilated and completely dry, and remove the water bowl for a little while after these products are applied. After painting or varnishing a cage and allowing it to thoroughly dry, turn cage heating devices to high for a few days before introducing a snake; heat further drives off solvent fumes. Polyurethane in organic solvent is notorious for leaking more fumes after cage heat is turned on.

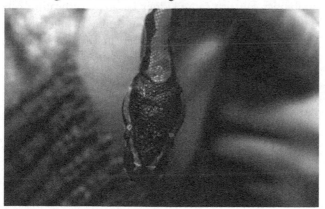

This snake recovered from a limp neck and hanging head after warmth and antibiotics, indicating that the source of the illness was either sepsis or bacterial toxins.

CHAPTER 11

SUDDEN DEATH

T he sudden death of an apparently healthy long-term captive is perhaps the most frustrating and puzzling event to snake keepers. There are a number of possible reasons, but only a necropsy will tell, and even then it may not always provide a clear reason. (See the discussions on psychological factors in chapter 14 and maladaptation in chapter 1.)

Parasites

One of the most common causes of sudden death in a captive snake is a parasite that penetrates the intestine and thereby causes internal bleeding and peritonitis. In many cases, this can be avoided by a regular fecal exam and deworming program.

Dehydration and Kidney Failure

Dehydration and kidney failure can also cause sudden death. A snake kept too warm and dry, consistently without sufficient water available, may die from uric acid buildup and eventual kidney damage. Past overdosage of certain antibiotics can also cause kidney failure. Overheating kills reptiles by denaturing enzymes and also by altering the metabolism in such a manner that life processes cannot continue. Overheating also causes rapid dehydration. Malfunctioning heating devices or thermostats are often to blame, as are empty water bowls and the absence of a moisture box.

Heart Disease

Heart disease has been determined to be more common in captive snakes than was previously thought. Overfeeding, combined with a lack of exercise results in obesity, high

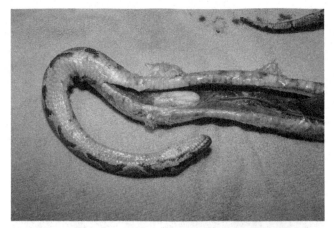

This snake died from gout and septicemia. Septicemia is one of the leading causes of sudden death in snakes.

cholesterol levels, and increased risk of a fatty heart. Small snakes are particularly susceptible to septicemia (high levels of bacteria in the blood, which commonly go undetected), which may develop and run its fatal course in a matter of days. This disease is frequently associated with filthy cage conditions. Larger snakes also are prone to septicemia, but the signs of infection may be less apparent.

Vitamin and Mineral Deficiencies

Vitamin and mineral deficiencies may result in the acute appearance of neurological symptoms, even though the problem is usually caused by chronic malnourishment. The appearance of neurological symptoms in fish-eating snakes, caused by a vitamin B deficiency, is such an instance. (See also chapter 10.)

Relocation

Long-term captives at one location may stop eating or die suddenly when switched to another location, even if ideal husbandry conditions exist. Typically, the reason for this situation is bacterial overgrowth in the gut, leading to gastroenteritis or septicemia; bacterial overgrowth is often related to stress, which causes immune system suppression. Veterinarians are generally wary of using antibiotics as a preventive measure, but in certain circumstances, as with new arrivals, snakes may benefit from a course of antibiotics

indicated by a fecal culture. You should also make every effort to provide a stress-free and clean environment for all snakes, especially for new arrivals.

Following Brumation

Sudden death immediately after brumation (hibernation) occurs in a similar manner. Some zoos have had massive die-offs of long-term captive snakes during such times. What appears to be happening is that the snake's immune response lags behind the rapid growth of pathogenic bacteria and protozoa. Death results usually within a week after the snake's emergence from brumation. If a snake shows any signs of illness or sluggish behavior following brumation, be prepared to administer metronidazole and amoxicillin orally and possibly amikacin by injection (follow your veterinarian's instructions). The dosages of these drugs are listed in the drug chart at the end of the medicine section. This entire disease process can be prevented by performing fecal exams and culture and sensitivity tests, then treating the condition or conditions accordingly, prior to transporting or brumating any snake whose health is questionable. Perhaps more importantly, avoid transporting or brumating any snake whose health is questionable. Only healthy animals should be brumated or shipped.

CHAPTER 12

PEDIATRICS

H erpetoculturists today are experiencing tremendous success in the captive propagation of numerous kinds of snakes, lizards, turtles, and crocodilians. As is the case with other animals and even with humans, the young of these captive-bred reptiles often have specific environmental and dietary needs that differ from those of their parents and may require specialized medical care. Fortunately, as herpetoculture has become more advanced, observations on the causes and treatment of medical problems specifically associated with neonate (newborn) snakes have increased dramatically; on the basis of these experiences, we can make some recommendations.

Birth, Hatching

In general, all neonates are subject to injuries to the umbilicus during the first several hours to days after live birth or hatching. In captivity, a young snake is especially susceptible to evisceration (gutting) if the umbilical cord becomes stuck

There are many medical ailments that can affect newborn snakes. Know how to care for them before they hatch.

to a nonporous surface such as glass, which can happen as the snake rests. When the snake moves later, the dried umbilical cord may pull the yolk sac and other viscera through the umbilicus, resulting in sudden death or fatal peritonitis. A substrate such as vermiculite or perlite (as used in the incubation box) or artificial turf usually works well during this period of several days while the umbilical cord dries out.

Feeding

After the initial period has passed, the young snakes will usually refuse to feed until they have shed for the first time, digested the rest of the yolk they have absorbed, or both. This process may take several hours in the case of very small snakes such as baby garter and ribbon snakes of genus *Thamnophis*, and brown and redbelly snakes of genus *Storeria*; it can take weeks in the case of larger snakes such as pythons of genus *Python*, boas of genus *Constrictor*, indigo snakes of genus *Drymarchon*, and pine snakes of genus *Pituophis*.

Young snakes may have dietary preferences that are very different from those of their parents. Most notable differences occur among the colubrids, especially kingsnakes of genus *Lampropeltis*, glossy snakes of genus *Arizona*, longnose snakes of genus *Rhinocheilus*, night snakes of genus *Hypsiglena*, crayfish snakes of genus *Regina*, and Australian pythons of genus *Liasis*. We are all too familiar with the juvenile gray-banded kingsnake (*L. alterna*), which has no interest at all in pinky mice (mice less than one week old) but will readily take lizards. The same can be said for most juveniles of all the aforementioned snakes. Indeed, there may be numerous other subtle differences between the dietary preferences and requirements of neonate and adult snakes. Fortunately, the young of most commonly maintained species of snakes will thrive on a diet consisting only of domestic mice of varying sizes. (For specific dietary preferences of all North American snakes, see Rossi and Rossi 2003.)

Smaller snakes have a number of other problems related to food and feeding. Generally, smaller animals

Each of these scarlet kingsnakes isn't much larger than a penny. These snakes should not be handled at all for six months and must be provided with a burrowing medium so they do not injure their spines.

have a higher metabolic rate. And even though reptiles are said to have indeterminate growth, they grow most rapidly during their first several years. Their small size also limits the size of the meals they can consume as well as their body fat reserves. Consequently, they generally require more frequent feeding than adults if they are to grow or even to maintain themselves.

Physical Environment

Smaller animals possess a higher surface-to-volume ratio than larger animals. This means that they are more prone to desiccation and overheating than their larger parents. Areas of high humidity and lower temperature within their cages are usually beneficial. A humidity box is one such area. These are plastic boxes that contain a moisture-retaining medium, such as sphagnum moss. Aside from preventing desiccation, these boxes are also very useful in preventing dysecdysis (see chapter 3) in young and old snakes alike. We also have found these high-humidity shelters to be very important for adults of the smaller snake species (Rossi 1992; Rossi and Rossi 1995 and 2003).

All of the other commonly accepted basics of herpetoculture including cleanliness, temperature gradient, clean water, good ventilation, proper substrate, and provision of some kind of shelter still apply, although modifications to accommodate the smaller size of the neonates may be necessary.

Competition

When all of the dietary and environmental requirements are taken into consideration, competition among the neonates may be devastating. Siblings housed together may compete directly with each other for food, basking sites, or areas of appropriate humidity. Overt aggression is also likely in some species but should not be regarded as the major indicator of competition among young snakes.

What appears to be a cozy pile of siblings sitting in a corner or basking on a log may be comparable to a group of people in a lifeboat! It is a collection of individuals that are packed together under the most stressful conditions and stay put because the surrounding environment may be even more hostile. Their presence in close quarters may increase their stress to the point that neither their immune systems nor their digestive systems can function properly, and some individuals may become sick. The immune systems of young animals are immature as it is, and such a living situation certainly is not beneficial. When juvenile snakes are kept in close contact, any disease of an infectious nature may spread rapidly among them and will more likely result in a higher rate of illness and death than it would among a similarly kept group of adults. It is for this reason that snake breeders have been successful using plastic shoe boxes to house their young snakes. Even though the young snakes do not have much room, they are housed individually. We therefore strongly recommend that you house neonates singly if possible. For example, it would be far better to house two neonate snakes in two 5-gallon (19-L) vivaria (assuming the enclosures are of appropriate size for the species) than it would be to house those same snakes together in one 10-gallon (38-L) vivarium.

CHAPTER 13
GERIATRICS

Herpetoculturists continue to learn about the care requirements of snakes in captivity. It is because of this growing knowledge that the life spans of these captive animals appear to be increasing steadily. Snider and Bowler (1992) listed a number of recorded longevities of various captive amphibians and reptiles. It is interesting to note that some snakes now have surpassed the forty-year mark in captivity. At this time, it appears that the pythons and boas are the snakes that live longest, with one boa constrictor living more than forty years and one ball python living forty-seven years. Other snakes—including some rattlesnakes, kingsnakes, and rat snakes—have exceeded thirty years in captivity. We still do

With proper care, your boa may live thirty years or more. Elderly snakes, like all animals, require special care.

not know whether these figures represent a bias in how many of each group is maintained—there are, for instance, many more boas in captivity than water snakes—and an individual's adaptability to captivity, or if the numbers are truly a reflection of natural life span. There also seems to be a relationship between size and longevity, as there is for many other groups of animals. In any case, more snakes are surviving longer in captivity, and consequently we will discuss the care of older snakes and some aspects of problems likely to occur in this older group.

Physical Observations

In general, snakes that have lived to at least fifteen years of age have been fairly trim, and none of them has been obese. It is strongly suspected that in snakes, as in mammals, obesity may relate to a number of other health problems, including heart disease and an increased likelihood for tumors. This is why we advise you to avoid excessive feeding of a captive snake. Vertical creases that form in a snake's sides indicate that a snake is becoming obese. If you observe these, less frequent meals of smaller size prey are advisable as well as a larger enclosure, which encourages activity. (See also chapter 7.) Snakes that are bred heavily (long term), may be prime candidates for obesity once their breeding slows down, particularly if they are sold to a novice snake keeper along with instructions to maintain the same feeding schedule.

Kidney Failure

Kidney failure has been observed in a number of snakes. It is often associated with overdosing of aminoglycoside antibiotics or chronic dehydration, but changes brought on by aging are a distinct possibility. Water should be available at all times for aged snakes, and their cages should never be excessively warm. The provision of a humidity box for most snakes may help prevent chronic dehydration and thus help prevent kidney disease. Large meals and heavy feeding schedules are not required by older, slow-growing senior ophidians. For these snakes, heavy feeding causes extra fat and extra work for their kidneys, which must excrete excess nitrogen.

Cataracts

Cataracts also have been observed in a number of older snakes. Cataracts associated with aging are not life threatening, because good vision is not essential for the feeding response of most captive snakes. Prekilled food will allow the snake, even an enfeebled one, to make better use of tactile and olfactory cues in securing meals. It is advisable, however, to rule out other causes of cataracts, such as diabetes, by checking with a veterinarian, who will collect blood to determine if there are any metabolic problems. We are just beginning to become aware of the geriatric problems of snakes. In time, much more specific recommendations will be possible. But for now, exercise good judgment and avoid the pitfalls.

Albino Snakes

One last interesting point: neither of us has ever seen an albino snake older than twelve years. Is this purely a coincidence, or is there some connection between albinism and shortened life span in these animals? Dr. Richard Funk (pers. comm.) suggests that fatty tumors are much more common in albino corn snakes than in other corn snakes. This may be an effect of intensive captive breeding, whereby adults are maintained on a high food-intake regime, or it may be a propensity associated with that particular morph.

CHAPTER 14

PSYCHOLOGICAL FACTORS

Stress reduction, disease prevention, and even treatment are intricately tied to creating the proper captive environment. The physical elements of this captive environment include water availability and proper heating, lighting, humidity, ventilation, and substrate. Research the details of the requirements of the particular species you keep. Psychological and social factors also play important roles in the keeping of healthy captive snakes, although these factors are often ignored. Handling, prey size and type (live or prekilled), visual stimulation caused by human activity, hiding places, cage stability, and the presence or absence of cage mates can all affect a snake's stress level.

This cage is too small for the snake. An improper cage environment can have pronounced psychological effects on snakes, which can ultimately lead to medical problems.

Use tongs to feed prekilled rodents rather than offering live food.

Handling

You must restrict handling, and even the visual stimulation of nearby human activity, of nervous animals. Covering the front of the cage with paper or cloth with only small holes in it will usually reduce escape behavior significantly. Placing the snake's cage in a low-traffic area is also beneficial.

Whether to handle a snake is a decision you must make on an individual basis. Young, fast-growing snakes (including most snakes intended for captive breeding) are best held infrequently, as they regurgitate readily when stressed by handling. Some animals may seem to enjoy handling, whereas others become extremely nervous when picked up. The presence of a cage mate may have a major impact upon the behavior of a snake. Commonly, one cage mate becomes dominant, and the other submissive. The dominant one thermoregulates properly and stays healthy, while the submissive one does not properly regulate its temperature and often suffers enough stress that it becomes sick. Indeed, the best way to house most captive snakes is to keep them singly.

Feeding

Always try offering prekilled food items first. This method has been tremendously successful in inducing feeding in recently captured snakes. Apparently, a dead food item is far less intimidating to most snakes, and because many snakes are scavengers in nature, they will usually consume prekilled rodents readily.

Privacy and Cage Stability

Providing a place in which the snake can hide is very important. This shelter, commonly referred to as a hide box, appears to be one of the most critical pieces of equipment in any snake's cage. It has been suggested that these boxes provide the security needed to improve appetite, digestion, and breeding behavior, as well as to reduce the likelihood of vomiting or regurgitation. Hide boxes perhaps increase the life span of some captive snakes by years.

Frequent vibrations that a snake may experience if its cage is placed on an unstable shelf may increase stress, thereby causing a loss of appetite. This long-term exposure to vibrations may possibly contribute to the demise of some animals.

Managing Aggression

Novice keepers commonly wonder why a snake suddenly becomes aggressive. The term *aggression* as we use it includes striking, biting, and constricting, and it may be directed either at a cage mate or at the keeper. Other actions, including vibration of the tail (regardless of whether the tail possesses a rattle), hissing, puffing up, close-mouthed striking, and playing dead are not usually regarded as acts of aggression in snakes, even though they may be preludes to aggressive behavior. Following are descriptions of some of the most common reasons for aggression in captive reptiles.

Some snakes, such as the one here, are naturally aggressive. Others become aggressive through conditioning, improper handling, hunger, or stress.

Hunger or Misdirected Feeding

A hungry snake will sometimes attack either a cage mate or its keeper. This misdirected feeding behavior is usually caused by olfactory or visual stimuli. The most common example is the snake keeper who has just handled a rodent and then attempts to handle a snake. The snake, smelling the rodent on the warm hand, may confuse the hand with prey and, naturally, strike it.

Competitive Feeding

Two snakes housed in the same cage may compete for food in a very aggressive manner. This behavior is referred to in wild animals as interference competition, and it certainly may be a factor in a captive environment as well. Tugs-of-war over food items are common in cages with many natricine snakes (garter and water snakes). In fact, the close quarters are likely to magnify these kinds of interactions.

Territoriality

Territorial disputes can become a common cause of aggression in captive reptiles. The animals may guard certain areas of the enclosure, such as shelters, basking sites, breeding places, or laying sites, or they may exhibit protective behaviors over food items. Recent studies have shown that snakes may be very territorial (Dr. Richard Franz, pers. comm.). Although aggression toward another member of the same species rarely has been observed in captive colubrid snakes, it is common in captive pythons (Ross 1990). Some herpetoculturists have observed fighting in indigo snakes housed in the same cage.

Sexuality

Recently, there have been a number of reports of aggression by adult male iguanas against their female owners at certain times during the owner's menstrual cycle (Frye, Mader, and Centofanti 1991). These reports suggest that the adult iguanas are responding to olfactory cues and are demonstrating displaced sexual aggressiveness. This kind of behavior has not been observed in snakes, but it is possible.

A keeper should never feed two snakes together as shown here. Shared feeding can result in tug-of-wars over a prey item or even the consumption of one snake by the other.

Behavioral Conditioning

Improper training can turn even a timid snake into an aggressive captive. We know of one snake keeper who always used to take her pet snake out of its cage, put in a live rat, then place the snake back in the cage. After several months of this routine, her timid snake bit her on the lip, arms, and elsewhere whenever she picked it up. The snake persisted in this behavior for months, and the owner was nearly ready to get rid of her pet. Then someone suggested that she reverse the process: feed the snake heavily while it was in the cage; wait several days and then, wearing appropriate protection, pick up the snake. Basically, the keeper had trained her snake to look for food when she picked it up, so when it found none, the snake became aggressive. This kind of behavior may be difficult to reverse. Some authorities have suggested that once snakes are established, you should feed them in cages that are separate from the cages in which they are normally maintained, thereby avoiding such problems.

Pain or Irritation

Pain brought on by parasites, toxins, or trauma may provide sufficient irritation to cause aggressive behavior. Typically, snakes agitated by such noxious stimuli will bite with far less provocation than snakes that are less irritated. We have seen very sudden onsets of aggressive behavior in snakes after they were infected with mites or certain protozoan parasites.

The time of shedding is also frequently associated with increased irritability in snakes.

Self-Defense from Improper Restraint

Some species are naturally aggressive. Many snakes, including venomous ones, may bite in self-defense. To state that snakes may bite out of fear would be a supposition, but sometimes they become aggressive when cornered, trapped, or restrained and no other alternative is available. Quick movement on the part of a handler sometimes seems to frighten snakes, and indeed this may be the case. Standing nervously in front of a snake for a long period of time while working up the nerve to pick it up also tends to upset some snakes. Firm restraint about the middle of a snake's body will often elicit a bite.

Normal Response of Wild-Caught Species (Pseudo Release)

Docile snakes living in captivity for years may suddenly become aggressive when they are placed either outside or in a different cage for a short period of time. Many owners have been bitten viciously by long-term captives that had previously never bitten after the snakes spent only a few minutes outside on the ground. This kind of behavior may be related to a number of factors, such as different lighting or temperature, but we suspect that these animals may "think" that they are wild again and respond as they would in nature to the approach of a large animal. We refer to this behavior as pseudo release aggression because it occurs in snakes that are otherwise docile.

Juvenile Hyperdefensive Response

Juveniles of most species seem to be particularly irritable and snappy, and many do not tolerate handling well. Some do. Apart from any learned behavior, the survival instincts of juveniles favor escape and avoidance because most young snakes are subject to attack by predators in the wild. In nature, when a juvenile snake is picked up, it is about to become dinner, not adored or purchased. For this reason, many young snakes may be very aggressive, but they usually mellow out with age, as they learn that their keepers mean them no harm. For lack of a better name, this has been referred to as the juvenile hyperdefensive response. Do not assume that all young snakes will remain aggressive indefinitely.

Overcrowding Irritation
Snakes crowded into a small area may be agitated constantly by physical contact with other snakes. This constant irritation may cause increased aggressive behavior, especially in more nervous individuals.

Sudden Temperature Changes
Elevations of ambient temperatures are known to affect the behavior of some snakes. Snakes handled at room temperature may be docile yet become extremely aggressive and bite repeatedly after they have been warmed up. In most cases, the aggressive behavior noted at the higher temperature is more likely to be the normal behavior pattern, while the apparently "peaceful" animal is one artificially subdued because of the lower temperature. At very high temperatures, aggressive animals may become lethargic again. When cooled off sometime later, their behavior may revert.

Summary
The causes of aggressive behavior in captive snakes are numerous. Improper handling techniques and poor husbandry practices may increase aggressive tendencies. Proper practices may reduce aggressive behaviors in many cases. We do not wish to overgeneralize about the innate aggressive tendencies of an entire species, but we encourage you to be aware that there are individual differences among snakes, just as there are among mammals. Much of this behavior may be learned, but some is innate. The widely held belief among herpetoculturists that captive snakes have individual personalities may have a basis in fact. The study of captive reptile psychology is as young as

is herpetoculture, and we still have much to learn. Medical problems certainly need to be considered in many cases of snake aggression. Your reptile-oriented veterinarian may be able to assist you in "unexplainable" cases of aggression.

Psychological factors affecting captive snakes are numerous. The nature of the animal itself plays a large part in how it adapts. Still, you need to be aware of some of the underlying factors that create stress in a captive snake and make every effort to minimize their effects. To do so, you must begin at the time of capture. Successful herpetoculture involves every phase of captivity, from transportation through housing and daily management.

CHAPTER 15

CHOOSING A VETERINARIAN

At the time of this writing, there are more than seventy thousand veterinarians in the United States. The vast majority of them have received superb training in the medicine of domestic animals, but few have received much training in reptile medicine. Being a cross section of humanity, veterinarians on the whole are individuals who are not particularly fond of snakes. Indeed, the best reptile veterinarians were herpetologists first. They often are aware of the natural history of their patients and can advise their clients accordingly. Because more than 90 percent of reptile maladies are related to an improper captive environment, knowledge of housing and care requirements is critical to treating these animals properly. We wish that one of these knowledgeable

Always choose a qualified reptile veterinarian to care for your snakes.

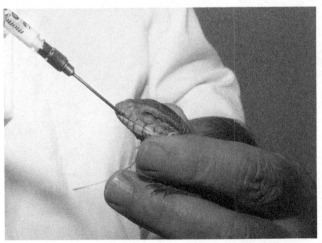

individuals could live near every snake keeper. Unfortunately, herpetologists-turned-veterinarians are rare, numbering perhaps fewer than fifty in the United States.

Another group of veterinarians who treat reptiles consists of individuals with a definite interest in and respect for reptiles and who have taken extra courses in reptile care. At least one of these caring and knowledgeable veterinarians can be found in most large cities.

A third group of veterinarians are very caring and helpful individuals who know very little about reptiles but will agree to help you, perhaps because no other help is available in your area. They may candidly admit that they don't know much about snakes but tell you that they'll get their books out and work with you to help your pet. These individuals can benefit tremendously if you bring them a copy of this book.

The last group includes those who do not work on reptiles at all and, worse, those who will treat reptiles without really knowing anything about their care. Fortunately, the latter situation rarely occurs.

Of course, you want to choose a veterinarian from one of the first three groups, ideally one of the first two. You can usually find the best reptile veterinarians by asking your neighbors, friends, local snake breeders, pet shops, zoos, museums, or a veterinary school. Another excellent source of information is your local herpetological society. A

Treating snakes requires specialized training and sometimes improvised equipment. Find a veterinarian who understands the special needs of your animals.

national herpetological directory has been published, and it may be available from your local public library or herpetological society. The veterinarian you choose should have a clean, well-equipped office and hold regular office hours with an appointment system, which usually creates reliable and timely office visits.

Laboratory tests for snakes may include X rays, fecal exams, blood chemistry and complete blood counts, cultures and sensitivity tests, and tissue biopsies. Good reptile veterinarians usually handle the snakes gently and take extra precautions with species known to be somewhat aggressive. They may have snakes of their own, and they rarely show fear of snakes.

A good reptile veterinarian should do the following for your snake: (1) ask what the problem is and take a medical history; (2) perform a complete physical exam; (3) perform the tests necessary to confirm a diagnosis; (4) encourage questions and discuss environmental or dietary corrections; (5) provide some literature; and (6) explain the fees.

In the last twenty years, major strides have been made in reptile medicine. A great number of research papers and books have been published about the medical care of reptiles. Recently, a number of veterinarians formed the Association of Reptilian and Amphibian Veterinarians, a group dedicated to the dissemination of information relating to the medical care of these animals. At the time of this writing, there are around one thousand members. Because of these advances, knowledgeable veterinarians can be tremendously helpful in saving the lives of many sick snakes and increasing the growth rates and productivity of breeders, much as they do for many other species. Pet owners and professional breeders alike have discovered that veterinary fees are usually wise investments.

CHAPTER 16

MEDICINES

O ur purpose in writing this book is to acquaint the reader with some of the common maladies of captive snakes, their treatments, and the critical nature of the captive environment. We cannot overemphasize that you should consult an experienced reptile veterinarian before administering antibiotics to a snake. In many cases, amateurs waste valuable time (and money) treating a snake with ineffective drugs or inappropriate doses. This delay may allow an infection to spread, resulting in the death of the animal. Another common outcome is that snakes may suffer kidney damage if they are overdosed. Be especially cautious about over-the-counter drugs available in pet shops. Many of these are not very effective and may delay the start of appropriate treatment.

The following charts list drugs that a number of veterinarians have found to be effective in treating snake maladies. Because many snakes are small (and many amateur keepers may miscalculate their doses), we include a chart especially for small snakes. If nothing else, the following

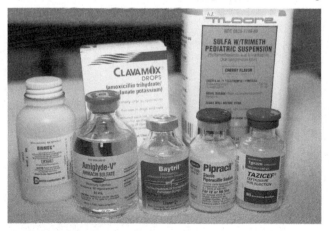

Never administer medications without consulting a qualified reptile veterinarian.

charts may help demonstrate how easy it is to overdose or underdose a snake. These charts can also serve as a quick reference for veterinarians who may be called upon to treat small snakes. The dose recommended in the first column is the dose with which we are most familiar and have used on a number of small snakes.

The drugs listed in the following charts are those most commonly used on snakes at the time of this writing. This is not to say that these are the only drugs being administered. For a more thorough discussion of antibiotics useful in all reptiles, consult Frye (1991) and Jacobson (1988). Note that the drug regarded at one time as the "miracle drug" for reptiles is not listed—we have not used Gentocin injectable for more than ten years and can find no benefit to using this drug as compared with the less nephrotoxic and broader-spectrum kanamycin derivative, amikacin.

The charts "Most Commonly Used Drugs" and "Small Snake Antibiotic Chart" include the doses of the drugs listed, calculated to the hundredth of a milliliter for the weight of the snake in question. For very small snakes, the necessary dilutions (with sterile water) of the standard drug concentrations are listed.

Problem/Solution Chart

Problem	Probable Cause	Solution
Anorexia/inappetence	1. Temperature too low 2. Prior to shed 3. Gravid female 4. Breeding male 5. Wrong food offered 6. Overcrowding 7. Psychological problems 8. Mouth infection 9. Intestinal infection 10. Respiratory infection 11. Parasites 12. Tumor 13. Too much handling	1. Increase temperature 2. Wait until shed 3. Wait until eggs are laid 4. Mate or wait 5. Offer different food 6. House singly 7. Add hiding places 8. See veterinarian 9. See veterinarian 10. See veterinarian 11. See veterinarian 12. See veterinarian 13. Stop handling
Bumps, lumps, blisters, sores	1. Cage too moist 2. Cage too dirty 3. Parasites 4. Abscesses 5. Burns	1. Keep dry; improve ventilation 2. Clean cage and disinfect frequently 3. See veterinarian and refer to drug chart 2 4. Incise and drain or see veterinarian 5. Check heat source and see veterinarian
Constipation	1. Humidity too low 2. Lack of exercise 3. Overfeeding	1. Increase humidity 2. Increase size of enclosure 3. Feed less and try warm water soaks and laxatives
Diarrhea	1. Parasitic or bacterial infection 2. Temperature too low	1. Deworm (run fecals) and see veterinarian 2. Increase temperature
Dysecdysis/improper shed	1. Relative humidity too low 2. Water not available or level too low 3. Mites or ticks 4. Injuries (old or recent) or infection	1. Increase humidity with humidifier or soak 2. Keep water available and deep enough for soaking when shedding 3. Treat parasites 4. Assist shedding
Failure to lay eggs	1. Not gravid 2. Mated later than thought 3. Egg-bound 4. Eggs reabsorbed	1. Mate again or wait 2. Check records 3. Provide laying box; increase heat and humidity, see veterinarian 4. Feed more, reduce stress, check for parasites, change brumation temperature, see veterinarian

Problem/Solution Chart

Problem	Probable Cause	Solution
Open-mouth breathing, throat puffing, bubble blowing, sneezing	1. Respiratory infection 2. Allergic reaction	1. Increase temperature and see veterinarian 2. Change substrate and clean and rinse cage; stop smoking around snake
Stomatitis (mouth rot)	1. Temperature too low 2. Trauma 3. Filthy cage	1. Increase temperature 2. Feed dead prey items 3. Disinfect cage; topical antibiotics; injectable antibiotics; see veterinarian
Vomiting	1. Too much handling 2. Increased stress 3. Temperature is too low 4. Parasitic or bacterial infection 5. Foreign body obstruction 6. Tumor	1. Stop handling 2. Cover cage; house singly 3. Raise temperature 4. Deworm; see veterinarian; run fecals 5. See veterinarian 6. See veterinarian
Wandering	1. Cage is too small 2. Hide box is too small or inappropriate 3. Cage is too hot 4. Hunger 5. Thirst 6. Mate searching 7. Undetermined cause	1. Increase cage size 2. Change hide box size, shape, opening 3. Lower temperature 4. Provide food 5. Provide water 6. Mate or wait 7. Use a smooth cage lid to protect snake's snout
Seizures, tremors, star gazing, weakness, paralysis	1. Vitamin B_1 deficiency 2. Septicemia (bacteria in blood) 3. Encephalitis 4. Toxicity 5. Parasite migration	1. Vitamin B_1 injection; see veterinarian 2. Antibiotics; see veterinarian 3. See veterinarian 4. See veterinarian 5. See veterinarian
Unusual swelling	1. Steatitis (inflammation of fatty tissue) 2. Cellulitis (inflammation of tissue) 3. Tumor 4. Gravid	1. See veterinarian 2. See veterinarian 3. See veterinarian 4. Prepare for egg laying or live birth

144

Most Commonly Used Drugs

Problem	Drug	Dose
Bacterial Infection		
	amikacin 50 mg/mL	2.5 mg/kg (0.0227 mL/lb) IM every 72 hours*
	enrofloxacin 23 mg/mL	5 mg/kg IM every 48 hours
	chloramphenicol	50 mg/kg SC, SID
	ceftazidime	20 mg/kg IM every 72 hours
	carbenicillin	40 mg/kg IM every 72 hours
	trimethoprim sulfa	30 mg/kg SC or PO every 48 hours
Intestinal Parasitism		
Amoebiasis	metronidazole (Flagyl)	20–50 mg/kg[†] PO[‡], 50 mg/kg commonly used
Coccidiosis	sulfadimethoxine (Albon)	90 mg/kg every other day for 3 treatments
Nematodes (hooks, whips, rounds)	ivermectin 10 mg/mL	0.2 mg/kg (0.01 mL/lb)[‡]
Cestodes and trematodes (tapes and flukes)	fenbendazole 100 mg/mL	50–100 mg/kg (23–46 mL/lb)[‡] or 25–50 mg/kg PO for 3 days.
	praziquantel 56.8 mg/mL	7.5–20 mg/kg (3–10 mg/lb)[‡]
Cryptosporidia	none effective (limited success with trimethoprim)	formalin and glutaraldehyde sufficient as disinfectants
External Parasitism		
Acariasis (mites and ticks)	ivermectin 10 mg/mL DDVP pest strips (Vapona)	0.01 mL/lb PO or SC or IM[‡] 3 hours every 3 days for 3–8 weeks; place on top of screen[‡]
	5% Sevin dust	Dust pillowcase and put snake inside case for 2–4 hours; dust cage also. Use carefully; ventilation is mandatory.

Important Note: Most antibiotics are used for a minimum of two weeks, but for some infections, much longer treatment is required; three to eight weeks may be indicated for some infections.

Note: IM = intramuscular injection; PO = by mouth; SC = subcutaneous injection; SID = once per day.

* 3–5 treatments usually

[†] *Lampropeltis* and *Drymarchon* species should not be given more than 50 mg/kg. Higher doses have been associated with toxicity.

[‡] Repeat in two weeks.

Deworming Chart

Drug	Fenbendazole	Praziquantel	Ivermectin
Concentration	100 mg/mL	57 mg/mL	10 mg/mL
Dose	50 mg/kg	5- 8mg/kg	.2 mg/kg
Dosage by Snake Weight			
1 lb/454 g	0.23 mL	0.04mL	0.01 mL
2 lb/ 907 g	0.45 mL	0.08 mL	0.02 mL
3 lb/1.3 kg	0.65 mL	0.12 mL	0.03 mL
4 lb/1.8 kg	0.90 mL	0.16 mL	0.04 mL
5 lb/2.3 kg	1.14 mL	0.20 mL	0.05 mL
7 lb/3.18 kg	1.59 mL	0.28 mL	0.07 mL
9 lb/4 kg	2.05 mL	0.36 mL	0.09 mL
10 lb/4.5 kg	2.27 mL	0.4 mL	0.1 mL
15 lb/6.8 kg	3.40 mL	0.60 mL	0.15 mL
20 lb/9 kg	4.54 mL	0.80 mL	0.2 mL
25 lb/11.3 kg	5.68 mL	1 mL	0.25 mL
50 lb/22.7 kg	11.36 mL	2* mL	0.5 mL
100 lb/45.3 kg	22.73 mL	4* mL	1 mL
Dosage Interval	Give once and repeat in two weeks and four weeks	Give once and repeat in two weeks and four weeks	Give once and repeat in two weeks and four weeks
Route of Administration	Orally	IM	SC, IM, or orally

Note: IM = intramuscular injection; SC = subcutaneous injection.

* One should probably not exceed a dose of 4 mL at one time. A dose this large should be divided into two or three injection sites.

Large Snake Antibiotic Chart

Drug	Ceftazidime	Amikacin	Piperacillin	Chloramphenicol
Concentration	100 mg/mL	50 mg/mL	200 mg/mL	100 mg/mL
Dose	20 mg/kg	2.5 mg/kg*	80 mg/kg	50 mg/kg
Dosage by Snake Weight				
10 lb/4.5 kg	0.9 mL	23 mL	1.8 mL	2.25 mL
20 lb/9 kg	1.8 mL	0.46 mL	3.6 mL	4.5 mL
30 lb/13.6 kg	2.72 mL	0.68 mL	5.44 mL*	6.9 mL*
40 lb/18.2 kg	3.64 mL	0.91 mL	——	9.1 mL*
50 lb/22.7 kg	4.54 mL	1.14 mL	——	——
60 lb/27.2 kg	5.44 mL	1.30 mL	——	——
70 lb/31.8 kg	6.36 mL*	1.59 mL	——	——
80 lb/36.3 kg	7.28 mL*	1.82 mL	——	——
90 lb/40.8 kg	——	2.04 mL	——	——
100 lb/45.4 kg	——	2.27 mL	——	——
150 lb/68 kg	——	3.41 mL	——	——
200 lb/90.8 kg	——	4.54 mL	——	——
Dosage Interval	Every 72 hours × 5 to 7 days	Every 72 hours × 5 to 7 days	Every 72 hours × 5 to 7 days	Every 24 hours × 10 to 14 days
Injection Site	IM	IM†	IM	SC or IM

Notes: Injection should usually be given in the front half of body. IM = intramuscularly; SC = subcutaneously.

* Certain drugs become impractical for large reptiles because of the large amount needed.

† A loading dose of 5 mg/kg is recommended. The loading dose is the first dose, which is twice the amount of the following injections for this drug.

Small Snake Antibiotic Chart						
Drug Concentration	**Enrofloxacin** (Baytril) 23 mg/mL		**Amikacin Sulfate** 50 mg/mL		**Ciprofloxacin** 10 mg/mL	
Snake Weight (pounds/grams)	Dose (mL)	Dilution	Dose (mL)	Dilution	Dose (mL)	Dilution
0.01 lb/4.5 g	0.01	1/10	0.025‡	1/100	0.05	1/10
0.02 lb/9 g	0.02	1/10	0.05	1/100	0.1 (0.01 if no dilution)	1/10
0.03 lb/14 g	0.03	1/10	0.075	1/100	——	——
0.05 lb/23 g	0.04	1/10	0.01	1/10	0.02	——
0.07 lb/32 g	0.06	1/10	0.015	1/10	0.03	——
0.09 lb/41 g	0.09	1/10	0.02	1/10	0.04	——
0.11 lb/50 g	0.11 (.01)	1/10	0.025	1/10	0.05	——
0.22 lb/100 g	0.22 (.02)	——	0.05	1/10	0.1	——
0.33 lb/150 g	0.33 (.03)	——	——	——	——	——
0.4 lb/181 g	——	——	——	——	0.2	——
0.44 lb/200 g	0.04	——	0.01	——	——	——
0.55 lb/249 g	0.05	——	——	——	——	——
0.66 lb/299 g	0.06	——	0.015	——	——	——
0.7 lb/318 g	——	——	——	——	0.3	——
0.77 lb/349 g	0.08	——	——	——	——	——
0.88 lb/399 g	0.09	——	0.02	——	——	——
0.9 lb/408 g	——	——	——	——	0.4	——

Small Snake Antibiotic Chart (continued)						
Drug	Enrofloxacin (Baytril)		Amikacin Sulfate		Ciprofloxacin	
Concentration	23 mg/mL		50 mg/mL		10 mg/mL w	
Snake Weight (pounds/grams)	Dose (mL)	Dilution	Dose (mL)	Dilution	Dose (mL)	Dilution
0.99 lb/449 g	0.1	—	—	—	—	—
1.1 lb/499 g	0.11	—	0.025	—	0.5	—
1.3 lb/590 g	0.13	—	0.03	—	0.6	—
1.5 lb/680 g	0.15	—	0.035	—	0.7	—
1.8 lb/816 g	0.17	—	0.04	—	0.8	—
2 lb/907 g	0.2	—	0.045	—	0.9	—
2.2 lb/1 kg	0.22	—	0.05	—	1	—
2.6 lb/1.2 kg	—	—	0.06	—	—	—
3.3 lb/1.5 kg	0.33	—	0.075	—	1.5	—
3.9 lb/1.76 kg	—	—	0.09	—	—	—
4.4 lb/2 kg	0.44	—	0.1	—	2	—
5 lb/2.3 kg	—	—	0.115	—	—	—

Notes: Ciprofloxacin is a broad-spectrum antibiotic that is often administered orally in snakes. It is one of the few antibiotics that are effective when administered to snakes orally. IM = Intramuscular injection.

* Recommended dose from literature is 5 mg/kg given IM every 48 hours. A loading dose (first dose) of 5.0 mg/kg is also recommended.

† Recommended dose from literature is 2.5 mg/kg given IM every 72 hours. A loading dose (first dose) of 5.0 mg/kg is also recommended.

‡ We have calculated doses one digit beyond the accuracy of the common smallest syringes (0.5 and 1.0 syringes). Round off to the nearest hundredth of a cubic centimeter (cc).

REFERENCES

Abrahams, R. 1992. *Ivermectin as a spray for snake mites. Bulletin of the Association of Reptilian and Amphibian Veterinarians* 2 (1): 8.

Boyer, T. H. 1992. Use of atropine for eliminating excessive mucus in boids. *Bulletin of the Association of Reptilian and Amphibian Veterinarians* 2 (1): 6–7.

Brown, C. W., and R. A. Martin. 1990. Dystocia in snakes. In *The Compendium on Continuing Education* 12 (3): 361–368.

Cowan, D. F. 1980. Adaptation, maladaptation, and disease. *Reproductive biology and disease of captive reptiles*, ed. Murphy and Collins. SSAR Contributions to Herpetology, 191–196.

DeNardo, D., and E. J. Wozniak, 1997. Understanding the snake mite and current therapies for control. Proceedings, Association of Amphibian and Reptilian Veterinarians: Houston.

Fitch, H. S. 1982. Resources of a snake community in prairie-woodland habitat in northeastern Kansas. In *Herpetological communities*, ED. N. J. Scott, Jr. U.S. Fish and Wildlife Service Research Report, no. 13:83–97.

Frye, F. L. 1991. *Biomedical and surgical aspects of captive reptile husbandry.* 2nd ed. 2 vols. Melbourne, FL.: Krieger.

Frye, F. L., D. R. Mader, and B. V. Centofanti. 1991. Interspecific (lizard:human) sexual aggression in captive iguanas (Iguana iguana). A preliminary compilation of eighteen cases. *Bulletin of the Association of Reptilian and Amphibian Veterinarians* 1 (1):4–6.

Gillingham, J. C. 1987. Social behavior. In *Snakes: Ecology and evolutionary biology*, 184–209. New York: McGraw-Hill.

Grier, J. W., M. S. Bjerke, and L. K. Nolan. 1993. Snakes and the *Salmonella* situation. *Bulletin of the Chicago Herpetological Society* 28 (3): 53–59.

Hammack, S. H. 1991. New concepts in colubrid egg incubation: A preliminary report. In the published proceedings of the Fifteenth International Herpetological Symposium on captive propagation and husbandry, edited by Michael J. Uricheck, 103–108. Seattle, WA.

Jacobson, E. R. 1988. Use of chemotherapeutics in reptile medicine. In *Exotic animals*, 35–48. New York: Churchill Livingston.

———. 1991. Reptile dermatology. In *Kirk's current veterinary therapy: Small animal practice*, 11th ed., 1204–1210. Philadelphia: W. B. Saunders.

Jarchow, J. L. 1988. Hospital care of the reptile patient. In *Exotic animals*, 19–34. New York: Churchill Livingston.

Junge, R. E., and R. E. Miller. 1992. Reptile respiratory diseases. In *Kirk's current veterinary therapy: small animal practice*, 11th ed., 1210–1213. Philadelphia: W. B. Saunders.

Klingenberg, R. 1991. Egg binding in colubrid snakes. *The vivarium* 3 (2): 32–35.

————. 1992. A comparison of fenbendazole and ivermectin for the treatment of nematode parasites in ball pythons *Python regius*. *Bulletin of the Association of Reptilian and Amphibian Veterinarians* 2 (2): 5–6, 49.

————. 2005. *Understanding reptile parasites*. Advanced Vivarium Systems. Irvine, CA.

Levell, J. P. 1992. Eradicating snake mites: A brief history with the report of another method. *Bulletin of the Chicago Herpetological Society* 27 (10): 205–206.

Lloyd, M. 1992. Vasotocin: The reptilian alternative to oxytocin. *Bulletin of the Association of Reptilian and Amphibian Veterinarians* 2 (1): 5.

Mader, D. R. 1989. Egg retention in reptiles. *The vivarium* 2 (5): 13–14, 23–24.

————. 1993. Obesity in reptiles. *Reptiles* 1 (2): 33–35.

————. 1996. *Reptile Medicine and Surgery*. Philadelphia: W. B. Saunders.

Mader, D. R., and K. DeRemer. 1992. Salmonellosis in reptiles. *The vivarium* 4 (4): 12–13, 22.

Paul-Murphy, J., D. R. Mader, N. Kock, and F. L. Frye. 1987. Necrosis of esophageal and gastric mucosa in snakes given oral dioctyl sodium sulfosuccinate. In the proceedings of the American Association of Zoo Veterinarians, 474–477.

Peterson, K. H., and R. Orr. 1990. An unusual mite infestation at the Houston Zoo. *Bulletin of the Chicago Herpetological Society* 25 (1): 10.

Qualls, J. M. 1989. A novel treatment for snake pneumonia. *The vivarium* 2 (1): 12–13.

Ross, R. 1990. Regurgitation syndrome in boid snakes. In the published proceedings of the Thirteenth International Herpetological Symposium on captive propagation and husbandry, ed. M. J. Uricheck, 81–85. Phoenix, AZ.

Ross, R., and G. Marzec. 1984. *The bacterial diseases of reptiles: Their epidemiology, control, diagnosis, and treatment*. Institute for Herpetological Research. Stanford, CA.

————. 1990. *The reproductive husbandry of pythons and boas.* Institute for Herpetological Research. Stanford, CA.

Rossi, John V. 1992. *Snakes of the United States and Canada: Keeping them healthy in captivity.* Vol 1: Eastern area. Melbourne, FL: Krieger.

————. 1996. Dermatology in reptile medicine and surgery. In *Reptile medicine and surgery*, 1st ed., edited by D. R. Mader, 104–117. Philadelphia: W. B. Saunders.

Rossi, John V., and Roxanne Rossi. 1995. *Snakes of the United States and Canada: Keeping them healthy in captivity.* Vol. 2: Western area. Melbourne, FL: Krieger.

————. 2003. *Snakes of the United States and Canada: Natural history and care in captivity.* Melbourne, FL: Krieger.

Rosskopf, W. J. 1992. Silvadene cream as a topical medication. *Bulletin of the Association of Reptilian and Amphibian Veterinarians* (2) 1: 6.

Seigel, R. A., J. T. Collins, and S. S. Novak. 1987. *Snakes: Ecology and evolutionary biology.* New York: McGraw-Hill.

Seigel, R. A., and J. T. Collins. 1993. *Snakes: Ecology and behavior.* New York: McGraw-Hill.

Snider, A. T., and J. K. Bowler. 1992. Longevity of reptiles and amphibians in North American collections. Society for the Study of Amphibians and Reptiles Circ. no. 21.

Suedemeyer, W. K. 1992. Use of chlorhexidine in the treatment of infectious stomatitis. *Bulletin of the Association of Reptilian and Amphibian Veterinarians* 2 (1): 6.

Todd, S. 1983. Vapona resistant mites? The *Herptile. Journal of the International Herpetological Society* 8 (3): 90.

ADDITIONAL READING

Association of Reptilian and Amphibian Veterinarians
http://www.arav.com
A nonprofit, international organization of veterinarians
and herpetologists founded in 1991. The organization
charges membership dues for actual participation, but the
Links/Resources page on the Web site can be accessed by
nonmembers. For membership information, visit the Web
site to download the form or write to:
ARAV
Attn: Wilbur Amand, executive director
PO Box 605
Chester Heights, PA 19017

Herp Vet Connection
http://www.herpvetconnection
This site provides listings to client-recommended
amphibian- and reptile-oriented veterinarians.

Kingsnake.com
http://www.kingsnake.com
An online community for amphibian and reptiles hobbyists. The site posts classified ads and provides message
boards and event listings, among many other resources.

Reptiles Magazine
http://www.reptilesmagazine.com
A monthly publication covering herps from A to Z.
The Web site provides useful care tips as well as links to
breeders, photo galleries, and message boards.

INDEX

A

abscesses, 31–33
acclimating, 27–28, 33–36, 98
aggression management, 132–36
albino snakes, 129
amikacin, 142
amoebas, 69, 117–18
amoxicillin, 78, 122
amphotericin B, 115
anacondas, 12
anal gland abscesses, 31
anorexia, 81, 87–91, 143
antibacterial ointments, 53
antibiotics, 141–42, 147–49; for encephalitis, 118; injecting, 30–31, 51, 57, 60; oral, 29, 58; post-ovocentesis, 105; systemic, 32, 58; topical ointment, 51, 60
antifungal ointments, 53
ants versus wax worms, 89
artificial turf, 54, 123–24
atropine, 113, 119

B

B_1 supplements, 82, 118–19
bacteria: gram-negative, 60–61, 78, 113; infections, 53–54, 113, 118, 145; sources of, 25, 27, 43, 78; transmission of, 24–27, 46–47; treatments, 30, 60–61
ball pythons, 5, 11–12, 68
behaviors, 34, 64, 126, 132–36
biopsies, 54
birth defects, 101, 105
bleach, 26, 46–47, 64
blind snakes (Leptotyphlops), 89
blood screen, 85
boas (Constrictor), 9, 11, 12, 116, 124
Boidae family, 11–12
breathing, 19, 75, 112–16
breeding. See reproduction
brumation, 88, 90, 99, 122

burns, 48–51, 143
burrowing snakes, 42, 88, 125

C

cage care, 26, 46–47, 64, 66–67
cages, 39, 88, 93, 130, 132
calcium gluconate, 103
Calphosan, 104
cancer cachexia, 86–87
captive-bred snakes, 8, 9, 12, 14
cataracts, 129
cedar shavings, 39
cerebral edema, 35
cervical dislocation, 16
chemical irritants, 112
children and snakes, 25, 28
chlorhexidine, 60–61
ciprofloxacin, 78
cleaning, 26, 46–47, 64, 66–67
cleft scutes, 105
cloacal region, 20, 100
cloth bags, 20–21, 22, 55, 65, 145
cloths, swallowing, 79–80
cobras, 69–70
coccidia, 69
Colubridae family, 11, 12, 14
competitive feeding, 133
constipation, 74–76, 91, 143
cool water soaks, 35–36
coral snakes (Micrurus), 69–70, 88
corn snakes (E. guttata var.), 14
cranial abrasions, 34
crash diets, 96, 97
crayfish snakes (Regina), 38, 124
crushing injuries, 57–58
Cryptosporidia, 28, 84
culture and sensitivity test, 30, 32–33, 52, 54, 73
curette, 31–32

D

death of snakes: autopsies, 26; causes of, 30–31, 33–35, 36, 62, 114; sudden death, 120–22
dehydration: causes of, 74, 77, 79–80; effects of, 80, 86, 92–94, 120, 128–29; treatments, 93–94
dermatitis, 52–54
deworming, 69–70, 79, 91, 146

dexamethasone, 36
dextrose, salt, and Ringer's, 94
diarrhea, 72–74, 143
diet: calories in, 84; fish, 74, 78, 81–82, 118–19; frozen foods, 25, 27, 57, 63–64, 74; for neonates, 124; preventive, 37; specific needs of species, 99; vomiting and regurgitation from, 77; for weight loss, 96–97; wild prey, 27, 63–64. *See also* feeding
dietary preferences, 81, 88–89
diseases and illnesses, 17–20, 37–38, 48, 96; good husbandry versus, 26–27, 37–39, 42–47; and metabolic rate, 84–85, 86, 91; from overheating, 35–36, 49; from transporting, 20. *See also* infections; injuries; parasites; *specific diseases and illnesses*
disinfecting cage, 26, 46–47
dorsal cranial abrasions, 34
drugs. *See* medicines
dysecdysis, 48, 54–56, 85, 143
dystocia (egg-binding), 92, 102–6

E

ecdysis (shedding): anorexia prior to, 90; and burns, 51; dysecdysis, 48, 54–56, 85, 143; prelaying, 108
egg-binding, 92, 102–6
egg care, 107–11
egg-laying box, 103, 107, 108
egg tooth, 111
electrolyte solution, 79, 93
encephalitis, 117–18
endocrine disorders, 85
enemas, 75, 103
enrofloxacin, 78
escapes, 13, 40–41
external parasites, 62–67, 145
eye caps, 55

F

fecal matter: appearance of, 17–18, 18–19, 74; examining during quarantine, 28; parasite tests, 25–26, 70–71, 73, 91, 115–16, 122

fecoliths (fecal stones), 74
feeding: after crushing injuries, 58; amount and timing, 83, 94–97; food preferences, 81, 88–89, 124; live prey, 56–57, 89, 90; neonates, 124–25; prekilled items, 131; scent transfer, 89. *See also* diet
feeding problems, 81–82; anorexia, 87–92; bacteria and parasites in food, 25, 27, 78; dehydration, 92–94; diarrhea from, 73; improper methods, 12; and lighting, 45; misdirected, 133; obesity, 95, 96–97, 106, 120–21, 128; from stress, 34–35; two snakes, one rat, 134; vomiting and regurgitation, 76–80, 144; weight loss, 82–87
fenbendazole, 68–69, 70, 91, 116
fertility problems, 99, 101
fish diet, 74, 78, 81–82, 118–19
fluconazole, 115
foam mats, 16, 17
force-feeding, 34, 88
foreign-body obstructions, 79–80
fox snakes (*Elaphe vulpine*), 14
full-spectrum fluorescent lights, 45
Fulvicin, 53
fungal dermatitis, 52, 53
fungal pneumonias, 114–15

G

garter snakes (*Thamnophis*), 14–15, 67, 86, 124
gastric wash, 73, 91
gastrointestinal problems: constipation, 74–76, 91, 143; diarrhea, 72–74; vomiting and regurgitation, 76–80, 144
Gentocin injectable, 142
Gentocin Ophalmic Solution, 60
geriatrics, 127–29
gestation period, 102–3
glossy snakes (*Arizona*), 124
glue boards, 40–41
gram-negative bacteria, 60–61, 78, 113
green anacondas (*E. murinus*), 8
gut atony, 113

H

handling snakes: after feeding, 77; examination, 17–20, 41, 59–60, 86–87; guidelines, 13, 15–17, 18, 19, 24–27, 70; improper methods, 12, 15, 135; restricting amount of, 131
hatchlings, 106, 110–11
heart disease, 120–21
heating devices, 43–44, 49, 50
heat packs, 44–45
heat-sensing pits, 19
herpetoculturists, 6, 13, 137
herpetologists, 6, 139–40
hide boxes, 42–43, 132
high-humidity retreats, 86, 125, 128
hognose snakes (*Heterodon*), 69–70
home treatments, 18, 28–32, 60–61, 73–75. *See also* medical treatments; veterinarians
hooknose snakes (*Gyalopion canum*), 115
hot rocks, 49
housing conditions, ideal, 33, 34, 37–39, 42–47. *See also* substrates; temperature
humidity, 43, 54–55, 74, 99, 125
humidity refuges, 86, 111, 125, 128
hunger, aggression from, 133
hydrogen peroxide, 60
hyperthyroidism, 85

I

identification methods, 23–24
illnesses. *See* diseases and illnesses
immunocompromised snakes, 31, 113, 122. *See also* parasites
inappetence, 81, 87–91, 143
inbreeding, 106
inclusion body disease (IBD), 28, 114, 118
incubation, 105, 106, 108–10
indigo snakes (*Drymarchon*), 69–70, 124
infections: bacterial, 53–54, 113, 118, 145; effects of, 52–54, 73, 77, 91, 117–19; encephalitis,

117–18; of reproductive system, 100; respiratory, 75, 113, 114–15; septicemia, 121; signs of, 59; sparganosis, 33; stomatitis, 59–61; viral, 114
infertility, 99, 101
injections: administering, 29–31, 93–94; of antibiotics, 30–31, 51, 57, 60; calcium gluconate, 103; Calphosan, 104; of fluids into injured area, 57–58; intramuscular, 30, 103, 119; intraperitoneal, 24, 79, 93–94, 104–5; of ivermectin, 65–66; subcutaneous, 113
injuries: burns, 48–51, 143; cervical dislocation, 16; escape injuries, 40, 56, 57–58; from improper injections, 29–31; from live rodents, 56–57; skeletal or spinal, 16, 58, 100; to skin, 56–58, 88; trauma from, 56–58, 88; of umbilicus, 123–24
insects, 27, 84
internal parasites, 28, 68–71, 145
intestinal impaction, 74–76, 79–80, 143
intracardiac catheter, 93, 94
intramuscular injections, 30, 103, 119
intraperitoneal injections, 24, 79, 93–94, 104–5
ivermectin, 18, 65–66, 68–69, 116, 119

J

juvenile hyperdefensive response, 135–36
juvenile snakes, 8, 10, 123–26

K

Kaopectate, 73
kidney failure, 86, 120, 128–29
kingsnakes (*Lampropeltis*), 14, 69–70, 116, 124–25

L

lactated Ringer's, 94
lighting, 45–46, 87–88, 100, 101
lizard preference, 89, 124
longevity, 86, 127–29

long-nose snakes (*Rhinocheilus*), 124
lumps, 143
lung parasites, 115–16

M

maladaptation syndrome, 33–35
maldigestion or malabsorption, 84
malnourished snakes, 19, 20
mating problems, 99–101
medical tests, 140; biopsies, 54; blood screen, 85; culture and sensitivity test, 30, 32–33, 52, 54, 73; gastric wash, 73, 91; tracheal wash, 116; X rays, 58, 80
medical treatments: abscesses, 31–33; burns, 50–51; dehydration, 93–94; encephalitis, 118; endoscopic retrieval, 79–80; enemas, 75, 103; examinations, 17–20; fungal lesions and infections, 53; intracardiac catheter, 93, 94; overheating, 36; pain felt by snake, 28–29, 134–35; respiratory infections, 113; sluggish behavior, 122; to stimulate appetite, 34–35; stomatitis, 60–61; suturing wounds, 58. See also home treatments; injections
medicines, 141–42; antibiotic, 147–49; deworming, 69–70, 79, 91, 146; most commonly used, 145; problem/solution, 143–44. See also specific medicines
melaleuca, 53
metabolic problems, 84–85, 86, 91, 117–19
metabolic rate and energy requirement, 95
metaproterenol sulfate, 113
metazoan parasites. See worms
methimazole, 85
metronidazole, 33–34, 69, 119, 122
Mexican vine snake, 7
mice, 63, 74, 75, 89, 90
microchips, 23–24
milk of magnesia, 75
milk snakes, 14, 85

mineral deficiencies, 121
mineral oil, 75
minnow traps, 40
minors, not selling snakes to, 13
mite-control products, 119
mites, 18, 19–20, 52, 62–63
mouse shy snakes, 90
mouth of snake, 19, 59–61
mucus in the mouth, 59
multivitamin injections, 34–35
mycobacterial granuloma, 32

N

Natricinae family, 11, 14–15
necrosis, 30
nematodes (*Rhabdias*), 115–16
nesting box, 103, 107, 108
neurological problems, 117–19, 144
night snakes (*Hypsiglena*), 124
nonresponsive bacterial pneumonia, 114–15
No-Pest Strips, 67
Nystatin, 53

O

obesity, 95, 96–97, 106, 120–21, 128
occipital condyle, 16
oral antibiotics, 29, 58
organophosphate toxicity, 119
origin of snake, 9
outdoor enclosures, 39
overheating, 35–36, 49, 72
oviparous snakes, 102, 106
ovocentesis, 103, 104–5
ovoviviparous snakes, 102
oxygen deficiency of embryos, 109–10
oxytocin, 104, 105

P

pain felt by snake, 28–29, 134–35
paramyxovirus, 114
parasites, 62, 63–64; *Cryptosporidia*, 28; effects of, 52–53, 73, 83, 120; external, 62–67, 145; internal, 28, 68–71, 145; lung parasites, 115–16; mites, 18, 19–20, 52, 62–63; pentastomids, 116; protozoan, 68, 69, 77, 79; sources of, 24–27, 28; sparganosis, 33; tests for,

25–26, 70–71, 73, 91, 115–16, 122; treatments, 64–67, 78–80; untreatable, 70
Pedialyte, 93
pediatrics, 123–26
pentastomids, 116
periorbital swelling, 63
personal hygiene, 24–27
photoperiod, 87–88, 100, 101
pillowcases, 20–21, 22, 55, 65, 145
pine snakes (*Pituophis*), 124
PIT tags, 23–24
Plexiglas tubes, 16, 17
pneumonia, 75, 113, 114–15
Polysporin ointment, 53
povidone-iodine ointment, 53, 60
povidone-iodine solution, 31, 51
powders for treating parasites, 65
praziquantel, 68, 69
pregnancy, problems with, 92
prelaying shed, 108
premating problems, 98–99, 99
privacy, 132
protozoan parasites, 68, 69, 77, 79
psychological factors, 130; aggression management, 132–36; and decreased appetite, 90; of feeding and handling, 131; privacy and cage stability, 132
purchasing snakes, 26, 27
pus from abscesses, 31–32
pythons (*Python*), 5, 11–12, 68, 108, 116, 124

Q

quarantine, 27–28; deworming during, 69; length of, 62; for mites, 18, 62–63; personal hygiene and, 24; on receipt, 22

R

rat bites, 56–57
rat snakes, 12, 14–15
rattlesnakes (*Crotalus*), 34, 89
recognition methods, 23–24
regurgitation syndrome, 77. *See also* vomiting/regurgitation
relocation, 121–22
renal portal system, 29–30
reproduction, 98; brumation, 88, 90, 99, 122; common mistakes, 106–7; dystocia, 92, 102–6; egg care, 107–11; gravid females, 92; mating problems, 99–101; postmating problems, 101–6; premating problems, 98–99
respiratory problems, 112–16, 144
reticulated pythons, 12, 116
rhabditiform larvae, 115–16
Ringer's, 94
rock rattlesnakes (*Crotalus lepidus*), 89
rodents: captive-raised, 27; mice, 63, 74, 75, 89, 90; nutritional value of, 81, 82; rats, 56–57, 75; two snakes, one rat, 134
rostral (nose) area, 19, 34
rosy boas (*Lichanura trivirgata trivirgata*), 11, 116

S

Salmonella, 28, 78
salt, dextrose, and Ringer's, 94
sand snakes (*Chilomeniscus*), 38
scarring, 51, 58
scent transference, 81, 89
selecting a snake: ease of care, 7–10, 12, 13, 14–15, 38; snake families, 10–12, 14–15
self-defensive biting, 135
sensory loss, 92
septicemia, 121
Sevin dust, 65, 67
sex of snake, 9, 31, 92, 95, 100, 101. *See also* reproduction
sexual aggressiveness, 133
sharptail snakes (*C. tenuis*), 89
shedding. *See* ecdysis
shovelnose snakes (*Chionactis*), 88
sight, sense of, 92, 100
sinusitis, 112
skeletal/spinal injuries, 16, 58, 100
skin, 19–20; injuries to, 56–58, 88; and longevity, 86; problems, 48–54, 143. *See also* ecdysis
smell, sense of, 92, 100
snake families, 10–12, 14–15

Snake Keeping Guidelines, 12, 13
snake mites. *See* mites
sparganosis, 33, 68–69
sphagnum moss, 107, 108
spinal/skeletal injuries, 16, 58, 100
sprays for parasites, 18, 65
starvation diets, 96, 97
steroid injections, 36
stomatitis (mouth rot), 59–61, 144
stools. *See* fecal matter
stress: causes of, 33–35, 103, 126, 130, 132; effects of, 73, 77, 121–22; reducing, 37
subcutaneous injections, 113
substrates, 39, 42; artificial turf, 54, 123–24; for burrowing snakes, 42, 88, 125; dehydration from, 55, 74, 91, 92–93; impactions from, 79; newspaper, 66; sphagnum moss and vermiculite, 107, 108, 109
sudden death, 120–22
sulfadimethoxine, 69
sunlight, 20, 22–23, 35–36, 49
swelling, 35, 63, 144
systemic antibiotics, 32, 58

T

tapeworms, 33, 68–69
Tech America, 119
temperature, 43–45; changes in, 77, 87, 136; and dehydration, 74, 92; and diarrhea, 73; and dystocia, 102; gradient, 37, 44–45, 49, 98, 100, 125; and infertility, 99; for mating preparation, 99; and metabolic rate, 84–85; monitoring, 23, 50; specific needs of species, 85, 99
terrestrial snakes, 11, 27
territoriality, 133
thermal burns, 48–51, 143
thermal gradient, 37, 44–45, 49, 98, 100, 125
thermometers, 23, 50
thiamine deficiency, 82, 118–19
topical antibiotic ointments, 51, 60
toxins, 117–19
tracheal wash, 116

transporting snakes, 13, 20–23, 35–36, 44–45, 122
trapping escapees, 40–41
trauma. *See* injuries
treatment. *See* medical treatments
tumors, 80, 86, 129

U

umbilicus injuries, 123–24
untreated wood, 74
uric acid in stool, 18–19
uterus, adhesion or torsion of, 105

V

Vapona-laden strips, 67
vasotocin, 104–5
venomous snakes, 17, 21, 40–41
ventilation, 43, 49
ventral scales, examining, 18
vermiculite, 107, 108, 109
veterinarians: choosing, 138–40; examinations, 25–26, 86–87; sexing, 100. *See also* medical tests; medical treatments; medicines; *specific maladies*
viral encephalitis, 28, 114, 118
vitamin deficiencies, 84–85, 121
vomiting/regurgitation, 76–80, 144

W

wandering behaviors, 144
water: dehydration from lack of, 92; offering, 22, 86, 103; soaking in, 35–36, 64, 75, 103
water snakes (*Nerodia*), 14–15, 67
weight loss, 82; anorexia, 81, 87–91, 143; causes of, 83, 84, 85, 86–87; and metabolic problems, 84–85, 86, 91. *See also* parasites
weight-loss diet, 96–97
West Indian boas (*Epicrates*), 12
wild prey, 27, 63–64
wild snakes, 9, 10, 27, 45–46, 135
wood fixtures or cages, 74, 92–93
worms: effects of, 52, 77; treatments, 69–70, 79, 91, 146; types of, 33, 68–69, 115–16
wounds, 56, 57, 58, 143

Z

zoonotic diseases, 24–27, 25, 116

ABOUT THE AUTHORS

Dr. John Rossi and **Roxanne Rossi** together have more than twenty years of experience in herpetology and herpeto-culture, particularly the captive problems of native snakes. John Rossi was awarded a master's degree in zoology in 1981 and a doctorate (DVM) in 1986. Roxanne Rossi has coauthored a number of articles with John on the subject and accepted the day-to-day care of more than 150 snakes representing more than 80 species of North American snakes.

CPSIA information can be obtained
at www.ICGtesting.com
Printed in the USA
LVOW02s0054260417
532188LV00007B/75/P